Arnulfo L. Oliveira Memorial Library

THE MATTHEW EFFECT

DANIEL
RIGNEY

THE
MATTHEW
EFFECT

HOW ADVANTAGE
BEGETS FURTHER
ADVANTAGE

COLUMBIA
UNIVERSITY
PRESS
NEW YORK

Columbia University Press
Publishers Since 1893
New York   Chichester, West Sussex
Copyright © 2010 Columbia University Press
All rights reserved

Library of Congress Cataloging-in-Publication Data
Rigney, Daniel, 1949–
        The Matthew effect : how advantage begets further advantage
/ Daniel Rigney.
            p.   cm.
        Includes bibliographical references and index.
        ISBN 978-0-231-14948-8 (cloth : alk. paper)
        1. Social stratification. 2. Equality. 3. Opportunity—Social
aspects. I. Title.
HM821.R54   2010
305.5'12—dc22
                                    2009021491

Columbia University Press books are printed on permanent
and durable acid-free paper.
This book was printed on paper with recycled content.
Printed in the United States of America
c 10 9 8 7 6 5 4 3 2 1

CONTENTS

PREFACE

THIS BOOK SEEKS to offer the general reader a clear and concise introduction to the Matthew effect, one of the least known but most important principles in the social sciences. Matthew effects are said to occur when social advantages lead to further advantages— or disadvantages to further disadvantages—through time, creating widening gaps between those who have more and those who have less. It has been more than forty years since the eminent sociologist Robert K. Merton of Columbia University coined the term to describe circumstances in which the rich get richer and the poor get poorer, as the saying goes. Matthew effects are not confined to the economic sphere, however; they have been observed across a broad spectrum of social institutions. Thus the principle is essential to understanding the social dynamics of inequality in general.

In the years since Merton coined the term, considerable research on Matthew effects has accumulated in fields ranging from sociology, economics, and political science to educational psychology and even biology. These widely scattered fragments of literature seem to point toward a fundamental principle in the social sciences, and yet they have never been brought together and presented as a coherent whole. This book aims to organize these fragments of research and present their major findings in a way that is readily accessible to social scientists, policy makers, students, and citizens at large as we continue to confront upward and downward spirals of inequality in the twenty-first century.

As a nontechnical introduction, this book does not require a strong quantitative background on the reader's part. For those interested in the more technical and mathematical aspects of Matthew effects, DiPrete and Eirich (2006) provide a useful review of the available literature and a good starting point for further research.

I gratefully acknowledge all the friends and colleagues who have helped to make this book possible. My dean, Janet Dizinno of St. Mary's University, and my editor, Lauren Dockett of Columbia University Press, have supported the project consistently along the way. I have gained valuable insights from the comments of Harriet Zuckerman, Joe Feagin, Brian Slattery, Richard Machalek, Bill Schweke, Roy Robbins, and several anonymous reviewers. I am grateful to Alejandro Parada for technical support. *Mi esposa*—the historian Alida Metcalf—and our sons Matthew and Benjamin have sustained me through this project with their laughter and love. They are my life support system. Finally, I wish to pay tribute to two luminaries of the past century, Robert Merton and Gunnar Myrdal, whose pathbreaking work continues to inspire thought and scholarship. This book is dedicated to their memories.

THE MATTHEW EFFECT

ONE

WHAT IS THE MATTHEW EFFECT?

WE ARE ALL familiar with the popular saying that the rich get richer while the poor get poorer. Though it oversimplifies reality considerably, the saying captures an important insight into the workings of the social world. In many spheres of life, we observe that initial advantage tends to beget further advantage, and disadvantage further disadvantage, among individuals and groups through time, creating widening gaps between those who have more and those who have less. The distinguished sociologist Robert K. Merton called this phenomenon the Matthew effect, from a verse in the Gospel of Matthew (13:12), which observes that "for whosoever hath, to him shall be given, and he shall have more abundance: but whosoever hath not, from him shall be taken away even that he hath."[1]

The existence of Matthew effects in social life may seem obvious. Yet the more closely we examine the phenomenon, the more complex and less obvious it becomes. In the first place, it is not universally true that the rich get richer while the poor get poorer—whether the riches in question are money, power, prestige, knowledge, or any other valued resource. Sometimes it happens that the rich and poor both get richer. Sometimes, as in deep economic recessions, the rich and poor both get poorer. And sometimes, though rarely, we find the rich getting poorer while the poor grow richer. Initial advantage does not always lead to further advantage, and initial disadvantage does not always lead to further disadvantage.

A host of vexing questions thus arise. Why and under what circumstances do Matthew effects occur, and why do they sometimes fail to occur? Why do we observe Matthew effects across such a broad spectrum of social settings, from economic systems to scientific communities and from schools to political institutions? Insofar as such effects produce growing inequalities within social systems, what are their moral and political implications? Matthew effects sometimes may produce socially beneficial results, but surely they may also produce manifest injustices, breeding resentment and even reactive violence among those who are left behind. Do we really wish to create a future in which the chasms that exist between the advantaged and the disadvantaged continually widen?

Finally, are Matthew effects and the widening inequalities they create beyond human control? Are they a law of nature, like gravity, which we simply must accept as inevitable? Or are they social constructs, created by human beings and thus susceptible to human choice and change? Can we control Matthew effects and their consequences, or must they inevitably control us?

Those who study inequality, or what sociologists call social stratification, have invoked a multitude of factors to explain how inequalities in the distribution of resources originate among individuals and groups. Some have argued that the rise of inequalities is largely attributable to differences in motivation, talent, and personal initiative. Others find the roots of inequality in brute force and the exploitation of the powerless by the powerful.[2]

The study of Matthew effects, however, is concerned less with the sources of inequality than with how these inequalities persist and grow through time. It explores the mechanisms or processes through which inequalities, once they come into existence, become self-perpetuating and self-amplifying in the absence of intervention, widening the gap between those who have more and those who have less. No theory of stratification is complete without attention to such processes.

The study of Matthew effects can have disturbing implications, especially for those of us who have enjoyed more initial advantages than most. We want to believe that the advantages we were born with, and whatever further advantages we have managed to accumulate in the course of our lives, are earned and well deserved. Meanwhile, we are surrounded on all sides by extreme social inequalities, not only in our own nation, but also within and among the nations of the world. If we are honest, we must acknowledge that some of us benefit personally from systems of inequality from which others suffer. Some part of us would prefer not to think about these issues; we may prefer to suppress these questions altogether, fearing that their answers will not profit us. Yet there is another part of us—some call it the social conscience—that activates a concern for the well-being of others and for the common good. That part of us, which Abraham Lincoln called the better angels of our nature, takes a special interest in how Matthew effects work, and will seek to know what, if anything, we can do to counteract their more destructive consequences.

Though we may be largely unaware of them, Matthew effects impinge on our lives and shape our futures. Most of us in advanced industrial societies are neither very rich nor very poor, but reside somewhere in the great gray middle. We may be advantaged in some respects—genetically, financially, educationally, socially—and disadvantaged in others. If we play our cards well, exploiting our advantages while mitigating our disadvantages—or if we are just plain lucky—Matthew effects may carry us in an upward spiral toward further advantage. On the other hand, if we play our cards poorly, or if unforeseen events, such as economic downturns, personal health issues, or family crises suddenly collide with our lives, the powerful undertow of Matthew effects may drag us downward. Sometimes neither our advantages nor our disadvantages are sufficiently great to set into motion either an upward or a downward spiral, and we find ourselves at a kind of break-even point, at which upward and downward effects roughly cancel each other out. But those who live in this great gray middle are continually vulnerable to the unexpected, to the uncontrollable, and to the impersonal mechanisms of Matthew effects. This book is primarily about the most advantaged and disadvantaged among us—the relatively rich and the relatively poor. But it is really about all of us, as we may all potentially encounter tipping points (Gladwell 2000) that sweep us either upward or downward into personal and social spirals. It is in our interest to understand how these

tipping mechanisms work and how they shape our lives for better or
for worse.

An understanding of Matthew effects and their social implications
is largely missing from current discussions of national and international policy. It is urgent that we raise awareness of the dynamics of
cumulative advantage, particularly in the face of recent policy initiatives—such as proposals for a return to more regressive forms of taxation and for the rollback of civil rights laws—that threaten to further
concentrate advantages in the hands of those who are already most
advantaged. Matthew effects are a missing piece of the puzzle that
must be set into place if we are to understand the deeper dynamics
of inequality in the world, both locally and globally. My hope is that
scholars, policy makers, students, and citizens at large will find in this
book a thought-provoking introduction to one of the most important
and least-known principles in the social sciences, and that they will
find ways to translate its insights into humane practice.

THE ORIGIN OF THE TERM

The term *Matthew effect* was coined by the Columbia University sociologist Robert K. Merton (1968a) to refer to the commonly observed
tendency, noted above, for initial advantages to accumulate through
time. Merton found that in certain social systems, initial advantages
are self-amplifying. Like the proverbial snowball that grows larger as
it rolls down a hillside, resources tend to attract and accumulate more
resources, which in turn accumulate still more resources. In his pio-
neering studies of prestige systems in scientific communities, Merton
demonstrated that prestigious scientists and institutions tend to attract inordinate attention and resources, leading to the further accumulation of prestige, which in turn attracts further resources.

As noted above, Merton borrowed his term from the Gospel of
Matthew (13:12), variations of which also appear in Matthew (25:29),
Mark (4:25), and Luke (8:18 and 19:26). All these verses observe that
to those who have, more will be given, while to those who have less,
even that will be taken away[3]—or in popular parlance, the rich get

richer and the poor get poorer. While these scriptural passages superficially may seem to refer to material wealth, their context makes clear that wealth is to be understood as a metaphor for the accumulation of spiritual understanding and the development of talents.[4] When we say that the rich get richer, we do not limit ourselves to considering material inequalities alone. As social scientists have employed the term, Matthew effects are not confined to the realm of economic inequalities, but may amplify inequalities of any kind in the distribution of valued resources, whether economic, political, cultural, or personal.

Merton first identified Matthew effects in the institutions of science, but similar effects are observed across a broad range of institutional settings. Scholarly literature on Matthew effects turns up in a remarkably diverse range of fields of study, including sociology and other social sciences, educational psychology, legal and policy studies, and even biology. There are surprisingly few explicit references to Matthew effects in economics—the field in which we might most expect to find them—but we do find closely similar concepts, such as economist Gunnar Myrdal's (1944; 1957) notion of circular and cumulative causation, to which we shall return.

Matthew effects are also implicit in cybernetics and systems theory, particularly in the concept of feedback loops. Early systems theory in sociology, especially in the work of Talcott Parsons (1951), focused largely on social processes that maintain equilibrium or stability in society. These processes are analogous to what cybernetic theorists call negative feedback loops (Wiener 1961 [1948]:97). Like the thermostat in your house or the homeostatic processes in your body, negative feedback loops moderate the behavior of a system around a stable state or set point. Matthew effects, by contrast, resemble positive feedback loops, which typically amplify deviations from set points and thereby destabilize systems—in this instance, by producing ever greater social inequalities. We will have more to say about feedback loops and nonlinear systems as our story unfolds.[5]

This book attempts to weave the scattered strands of literature on Matthew effects into a coherent whole to demonstrate their prevalence and significance across social institutions. In doing so, we go beyond Merton's work to account for more than forty years of multidisciplinary scholarship that has accumulated since Merton first proposed the concept. Chapter 2 considers the dynamics of cumulative advantage in the fields of science and technology. Chapter 3 examines their significance in economic systems; Chapter 4 in politics and public policy; and Chapter 5 in education and other cultural spheres. Finally, Chapter 6 considers some moral and political implications of self-amplifying advantage. There, we ask whether the Matthew effect might rightly be regarded as a social-scientific law influencing the behavior of social systems in general, or whether it is better understood as a social construct that we can choose to counteract if we have the moral and political will to do so.

THE PARABLE OF THE MONOPOLY GAME

To clarify the concept of the Matthew effect, it may be useful to begin with a modern parable. In the board game of Monopoly, all players begin with equal resources. Yet equal opportunity at the start soon gives way to extreme inequalities in the distribution of resources. Though there may be ups and downs along the way, the richer players tend to get richer, and the poorer players poorer, until eventually the richest player has monopolized all resources and the poor are left with nothing at all. As successful players accumulate income-producing property through a combination of skill and luck, their cumulative advantages allow them to reinvest new income in accumulating still more property, producing still more new income. This snowballing pattern of self-amplifying accumulation results in a Matthew effect that ultimately allows the most advantaged player to crush all opponents.

The sociologist Leonard Beeghly (1989) invites us to imagine a slight variation on the game of Monopoly that more nearly resembles real life. In Beeghly's version, each player begins with a different sum of money. Let us suppose hypothetically that some players begin the game with $5,000, others begin with $1,000, and still others with only $500. Those who begin with $5,000 enjoy a considerable head start on the competition. They can well afford to acquire every property they land on, and they soon own a disproportionate share of the income-producing properties on the board. Those who follow after them are less able to afford properties of their own, and instead usually find themselves spending their limited resources in rent payments, enriching the large owners and impoverishing themselves in the process. The laws of probability virtually ensure that under these conditions, the rich will get richer and the poor poorer, and through no special virtue or vice of their own. Initial advantages are parlayed into greater advantages, creating a widening gap between haves and have-nots—or, more precisely, between have-mores and have-lesses—through time.

It is true that everyone has some degree of opportunity to succeed in such a game, however small that chance may be, and in rare instances, a player who begins with fewer resources may win through some combination of luck and skill. But it is a statistical fallacy to claim that rich and poor players have an equal opportunity to succeed. The rules and initial conditions of the game virtually guarantee that inequalities widen as the game progresses, even among players who are identical to each other in every respect except initial monetary advantage. When two identical twins with the same level of talent and effort play this version of Monopoly against each other, the twin who begins with more resources almost always wins.

In many ways, American society resembles the skewed Monopoly game described above. Like skewed Monopoly, American society is a highly competitive system driven largely by the pursuit of material success, and participants begin with vastly differing resources. Yet despite these vast inequalities of initial condition, and despite the obvious advantages that these initial conditions confer upon the more privileged, many Americans remain steadfast in the conviction that ours is indeed a land of equal opportunity. They fail to distinguish between the statements that everyone in America has an opportunity to succeed and that everyone in America has an *equal* opportunity to succeed.

The first statement is undeniably true. The second is profoundly and demonstrably false. In the United States or any other modern society, the probability of going from rags to riches exists, and one may produce carefully selected anecdotes to prove that this is commonplace. But in reality, the probability of going from rags to riches—or from riches to rags—is miniscule compared to the probability of going from riches to riches, or from rags to rags. Highly selective and unrepresentative anecdotes only obscure the larger statistical truth of the matter: Though some social mobility does occur, those who begin life with substantial advantages generally fare much better, on average, than those who do not.

As the old baseball joke has it, some begin life with two strikes against them while others are born on third base and think they've hit a triple. And while the former may reach home in some instances, and the latter may fail to do so, the probabilities overwhelmingly favor the latter over the former, as any good baseball statistician will verify. The respective chances of the two players are not even remotely equal, even when the two players are exactly equal in talent and drive. Would any rational and informed person seriously argue that the son or daughter of a billionaire and the son or daughter of a migrant farm worker share anything even remotely approaching an equal opportunity to acquire material wealth? Yet many among us seem implicitly to believe that this is the case, and grow hostile at the mere suggestion that it may be patently untrue.

ABSOLUTE VERSUS RELATIVE MATTHEW EFFECTS

The game of Monopoly is a particularly clear example of what we might call absolute Matthew effects. The rich get absolutely richer while the poor get absolutely poorer and eventually go bankrupt. But we may also speak of relative Matthew effects, which occur when the rich and poor both get richer, but the rich get richer by a larger margin, creating a widening gap between themselves and the poor. This latter type may be neatly illustrated through the familiar concept of compound interest. Suppose that you and I both deposit our money in a bank that generously offers (let us say for the sake of easy calculation) a 10 percent annual rate of interest on our deposits. Further suppose that I have $1,000 to deposit, while you have only $100. Thus the initial gap between us stands at $900. Now suppose that we track our respective bank accounts over time, reinvesting our interest by adding it to our accumulated principal compounded annually. By the end of the first year, I have $1,100 and you have $110. We have both grown richer by 10 percent, but the gap between our respective accounts has widened from $900 to $990. Over time, the size of this gap widens at an accelerating rate, so that by the end of ten years, I have $2,594 in my account and you have only $259 in yours. An initial difference of $900 is now a difference of $2,335. After 100 years, my account holds nearly $14 million and yours nearly $1.4 million. The ratio of my account to yours remains constant at 10 to 1, but the gap between the two stands at more than $12 million. We have experienced the same percentage growth in our initial investments. But wealth and buying power are not measured in percentage points; they are measured in units of currency, and in that regard, I have gained vastly more than you have, and through no moral virtue of my own. I have merely ridden the mathematical wave of the Matthew effect.

The example of compound interest illustrates a relative Matthew effect: Both accounts grow at the same rate, yet because my gains on a larger base vastly exceed yours, the gap between us widens dramatically over time. The gap widens even more rapidly when, as often happens in the real world of finance, those who begin with more receive a higher rate of return on their investments than those who begin with less.

Thus far, we have considered compound interest only from the point of view of the investor. Big investors stand to gain more from compound interest than small investors do. Now consider the situation from the perspective of the debtor, whose interest payments on the unpaid balance of a loan are also compounded, and whose compounded losses make the lender's compounded gains possible. As Boshara (2003:94) observes, "wealth, like debt, is self-replicating. Compound interest turns wealth into more wealth and debt into more debt." The lender grows richer while the debtor grows poorer—especially if the debtor borrows from a predatory lender and sinks even more deeply into debt. In such real life circumstances, the gap between rich and poor widens even more rapidly than in the previous example, producing not merely a relative but an absolute Matthew effect. As the appendix shows, something similar to this has occurred in many developing countries, as they have sunk ever more deeply into debt to banks in the developed world and cannot pay even the interest on their loans, let alone repay the principal. Developed countries themselves are not immune to the hazards of compound debt. The national debt in the United States currently exceeds $10 trillion, with the rapidly expanding interest on this debt to be repaid, theoretically, by future generations. The dynamics of compound interest and compound debt are illustrated in the accompanying figure.

The opposite of a Matthew effect is observed when the rich get poorer while the poor get richer. Historically, such effects are considerably rarer than Matthew effects, but they may occur when upper classes are brought down (through violent or peaceful means) and their resources are redistributed among the have-nots. In this instance, the gap between rich and poor narrows—that is, if the rich are not liquidated along with their assets. Finally, the rich and poor may grow poor together at varying rates, as can occur during economic depressions, when the total size of the economic pie shrinks and every stratum of society receives a smaller piece.

As we reflect further upon these types, we realize that there are actually six possible subtypes, or patterns of relations, between those who have more and those who have less when we account for the rates at which individuals or groups become richer or poorer. Let us leave aside for the moment those who are neither rich nor poor but somewhere in between, and consider only those at either extreme. When we compare the resources of two individuals or groups at two points in time, we may find any of the following scenarios:

THE GAP BETWEEN RICH AND POOR WIDENS WHEN . . .

1. The rich get richer while the poor get poorer, creating an absolute Matthew effect;

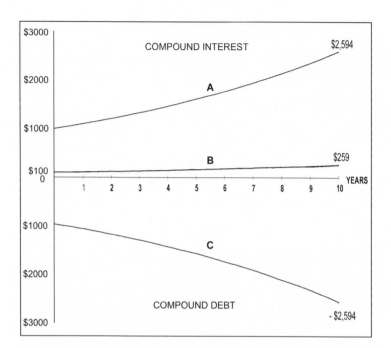

ABSOLUTE AND RELATIVE MATTHEW EFFECTS

The figure illustrates relative and absolute Matthew effects using compound interest and debt as examples. Line A represents an investor who deposits $1,000 for ten years at a hypothetical 10 percent rate of interest, compounded annually. Line B represents an investor who has only $100 to invest at the same rate. The relationship between A and B illustrates a relative Matthew effect. Both investors gain after ten years and the ratio of their respective gains remains constant at 10:1, but investor A's gains are far larger as the monetary gap between A and B widens from $900 to $2,335. Line C represents a borrower who cannot repay the principal on a $1,000 loan and is assessed annual interest and fees amounting to 10 percent compounded annually. The relationship between A (or B) and C illustrates an absolute Matthew effect, wherein the more advantaged gain while the less advantaged fall farther behind, in not only relative but absolute terms.

2. The rich get richer while the poor get richer at a slower rate, creating a relative Matthew effect;
3. The rich get poorer while the poor get poorer at a faster rate.

THE GAP BETWEEN RICH AND POOR NARROWS WHEN . . .

4. The rich get poorer while the poor get poorer at a slower rate.
5. The rich get richer while the poor get richer at a faster rate.
6. The rich get poorer while the poor get richer—the opposite of an absolute Matthew effect.

To understand the distinction between absolute and relative effects more clearly, we must understand what game theorists call zero-sum games. In a zero-sum game, the sum total of available resources is a fixed quantity. In this closed system, any gain made by one player can only be had at the expense of other players. If we add the gains of the winners and the losses of losers, the sum is zero—hence the term. In a zero-sum game, there can be no relative Matthew effects, no win-win outcomes wherein both rich and poor make gains. Thus economist Lester Thurow (1980) worried that, during periods of economic stagnation, all segments of society would fight over a fixed quantity of economic pie, resulting in socially destructive conflicts. Even more socially destructive would be a negative-sum situation, such as an economic depression, wherein all segments of society must fight for pieces of a shrinking pie.

Contrast the closed system with an open system, in which available resources are expanding. In this positive-sum scenario, relative Matthew effects and win-win outcomes are possible though not inevitable, as one or another player may attempt to monopolize the gains. Something like this appears to have happened in the United States from 1977 to 1989, when 60 percent of national gains in after-tax income (and 77 percent of gains in pre-tax income) found their way into the pockets of the richest 1 percent of the population (Nasar 1992). As the appendix shows, the story of the American economy over the past thirty years largely has been a tale of growing accumulation of wealth and income at the top, with modest gains among middle-income groups and relative stagnation or absolute decline among the poor.

THE MATTHEW EFFECT IN MERTONIAN THEORY

Before we launch into an analysis of Matthew effects in science, economy, politics, and education, let us first deepen our understanding of the concept by considering its connection to other important concepts in social theory. The recognition of Matthew effects is not, after all, an isolated insight into the workings of the social world; it is an integral part of a complex network of ideas and their relationships, which Robert K. Merton developed throughout the course of his illustrious career. Three concepts in particular are essential to understanding the place of the Matthew effect in the larger corpus of Merton's social theory.

UNINTENDED CONSEQUENCES

First, Mertonian theory emphasizes that social actions often have unintended consequences (1936; 1968b). In a retrospective essay, Merton described the phenomenon of unintended consequences as an "enduring interest" in his intellectual life and a "core idea" from which other important concepts emanated. As a theorist in the functionalist tradition, Merton was interested not only in the subjective motives and intentions of social actors, but also in the objective functions or consequences of their actions for the sustainability of the social or cultural systems within which they occur. He believed that social and cultural systems are the products not of conscious design alone, but of unintended processes of social evolution as well (1998:304).

Merton (1968b:104–05) made an important distinction between manifest and latent functions. A function or consequence of a social phenomenon is said to be manifest if it is intended and recognized by system participants, but latent if it is unintended and unrecognized. Merton introduced a bit of confusion at this point when he conflated consequences that are intended or unintended with those that are recognized or unrecognized. Hypothetically, a consequence could be intended but unrecognized, or recognized but unintended. Here, we focus not on whether the consequences of a given social phenomenon are recognized, but rather on whether they are intended, and whether such consequences are positive (functional) or negative (dysfunctional) for the sustainability of the social system as a whole. When Gottlieb Daimler invented one of the earliest gasoline-powered automobiles in 1886, he and others clearly intended and recognized that it would transport passengers from one place to another more rapidly than the horse and buggy could. The automobile's primary manifest function was to make transportation more efficient. Daimler probably did not intend or recognize, however, that his invention would have a multitude of other positive and negative consequences as well: It would usher in an era of drive-ins and drive-throughs, freeways and suburbs, petroleum dependence and climate change. For Daimler and those living in his day, these would have been latent functions or dysfunctions of the automobile.

We may take several lessons from the automobile's example. First, we cannot seem to do just one thing; virtually every social act has multiple consequences. The social impact of the automobile has radiated outward in all directions from its point of origin, influencing virtually every aspect of our lives for better and worse. Second, the consequences of social action are not only multiple, but often ambiguous and even contradictory. On the one hand, automobiles have brought us closer together by shrinking the temporal distances among us. On the other hand, they have also simultaneously created greater social distances among us by locking us into isolated moving compartments and allowing us to escape each other at ever greater speeds. Finally, whether one deems the consequences of social action to be positive or negative for society depends in part upon one's own values and interests, resulting in varied understandings of what constitutes the true or desired nature of the social system in question. Freeways and suburbs, which most Americans once regarded as desirable, are now seen increasingly as mixed blessings at best and accursed at worst. Whether petroleum dependency is a positive or a negative consequence of the automobile may depend on whether one works for an oil company or an environmental defense organization. Thus, when we say that a given social practice is functional, helping to sustain a given society, we must always ask for whom it is functioning well. What kind of society are we trying to sustain, whose interests are to be served, and in what time horizon? The internal-combustion automobile, however functional it may have been for many in the industrial societies of the past, appears to be increasingly dysfunctional for the long-term sustainability of the postindustrial societies of the future.[6]

What has all this to do with Matthew effects? Are such effects intended or unintended, and are they functional or dysfunctional for the sustainability of the social structures in which they occur?

Let us take the first question first. Do social actors consciously design systems in such a way that they systematically favor those who are already advantaged and disfavor those who are not? In other words, are Matthew effects intentionally designed into social systems? We would be naïve not to acknowledge that such intentional design sometimes occurs. The cynic's golden rule—that those who have the gold make the rules—suggests that dominant groups often enjoy the power to design systems from which they themselves will accumulate further benefits.

There are limitations, however, to this rather conspiratorial view of the origin of Matthew effects. Social systems are not entirely the product of conscious design. Every social institution is in some measure an accumulation of unintended and undesigned accretions. Complex social institutions, such as religious and legal systems, evolve over the course of many centuries, reflecting the contributions of countless individuals and groups of diverse ideologies, often working at cross purposes with each other. If Matthew effects are found in these systems, can such effects be neatly ascribed to the self-interested machinations of their master designers? Or are the effects sometimes better understood as products of social evolution, the systemic properties of which are largely unintended and even unrecognized by system participants?

The position advanced here is that the intentionality of Matthew effects must be judged on a case-by-case basis, with close attention to the particularities of the system under investigation. We may judge that politically engineered tax reforms conferring further advantages on those who are already advantaged—plainly speaking, tax cuts for the rich—are products of intentional and self-interested design. On the other hand, widening disparities in the performances of school children are almost certainly not the intended outcomes of educational systems, but rather unintended consequences. When Merton investigates Matthew effects in the allocation of status rewards in science, he does not argue that the effects have been engineered consciously into the apparatus of scientific work. Instead, he analyzes such effects primarily as latent functions and dysfunctions in the normal operation of scientific institutions; to use his phrase, they are largely "unanticipated and unintended" (Merton 1988:615).

Are Matthew effects functional or dysfunctional for the operation of the social structures in which they occur? In the context of his analysis of scientific reward systems, Merton clearly answers that they are both (Dannefer 2003). Merton's thought reflects an acute awareness of the intricate complexities, ironies, ambiguities, and multivalences of social life. Thus, in his study of elite scientists, he recognizes the positive functions that cumulative advantage performs in scientific communities, facilitating talent recognition and the maintenance of quality standards, while at the same time acknowledging that cumulative advantage can also breed dysfunctional talent suppression, inequity, and resentment among the ranks of well-qualified but lesser-known scientists.

Perhaps the most influential analysis of the positive functions of social inequality has been that of Davis and Moore (1945), who find inequalities in the distribution of rewards across all human societies. This suggests that some measure of inequality is functionally necessary for societal survival. Davis and Moore seek to explain this cultural universal by invoking two factors: the functional importance of positions in society and the scarcity of personnel available to fill them. They reason that some positions in society are more functionally important to societal survival than others. Not everyone has the talent and training to fill these positions competently, and so it is necessary to confer greater rewards upon those who possess the skills and are willing to make the sacrifices needed to fill them capably. The resulting inequalities benefit society as a whole, the authors argue, ensuring that the most capable people perform the most socially important tasks.

Critics of the Davis-Moore theory of stratification have responded that it understates the negative consequences or dysfunctions of stratification for society. Melvin Tumin (1953) has led the charge, challenging each of Davis and Moore's principal arguments point by point. He notes that elites often restrict access to privileged positions and suppress the potential talent of those below them in ways that serve their own elite interests (an instance of the Matthew effect). Their privileged positions give them the political power needed to promote self-serving ideologies that rationalize their interests as "'logical,' 'natural' and 'morally right.'" The resulting inequities are likely to breed hostility and resentment among the suppressed, leading to social unrest and instability. These and other dysfunctional consequences of stratification undermine the view that inequalities in human societies are unequivocally beneficial to society as a whole.

Merton's own stance employs elements of both these opposing views, acknowledging both positive and negative functions in the operation of Matthew effects in the reward system of science. While this book will give more attention to the dysfunctions of Matthew effects than Merton might have (I am tempted to describe the theoretical stance of the book as *dysfunctionalism*), his scholarship is a constant reminder of the need for a balanced appreciation of the many-sided complexities of social life, which defy ideological reduction.

OPPORTUNITY STRUCTURES

Merton's concept of opportunity structure is another essential key to understanding Matthew effects. Merton (1995a:25) defines opportunity structure as "the scale and distribution of conditions that provide various probabilities for acting individuals and groups to achieve specifiable outcomes." Opportunities are not distributed randomly in social systems, except perhaps in the rare case of universal lotteries; they are distributed in ways that favor some over others. Thus, those who are variously located in the social structure have varying degrees of access to the things they aspire to—aspirations which may include but are not limited to economic advantage and social mobility (1995a:6, 20).

Opportunity structures, and access to them, are not static; they may expand or contract for different individuals or groups at different times and places in history. The G.I. bill in the aftermath of World War II dramatically expanded access to the educational opportunity structure for veterans who might not otherwise have contemplated the expensive option of going to college (Merton 1995a:18). Similarly, the civil rights legislation of the 1960s expanded access to structures of civic and economic opportunity for entire categories of Americans who had previously been systematically denied such access. But while one's location in the social structure strongly influences the extent of access to opportunity, it does not wholly determine social outcomes. Access to opportunity merely enhances the probabilities or chances of achieving success. In Merton's conceptualization, an important place remains for human agency and choice. It is not only the opportunities to which social actors have access that matters, but what they do with these opportunities. In the language of social theory, our lives are the products of structure, agency, and the subtle interplay of the two. The subjective perceptions, expectations, and motivations of social actors affect how they adapt and respond to the structural opportunities and barriers they encounter (Merton 1995a:17; Marwah and Defleur 2006) and, hence, play a part in shaping their objective outcomes.

Merton (1938) began to develop the concept of opportunity structures in his influential theory of deviance, in which he argued that deviant behavior often results when individuals or groups are deprived of socially legitimate access to culturally defined goals, such as material success. Merton's theory of deviance has often been invoked to account for the emergence of criminal organizations and delinquent subcultures among economic and ethnic groups in American society whose access to socially legitimated pathways of upward mobility has been blocked by more advantaged groups. Building on Merton's theory of deviance, Cloward and Ohlin (1960:86) hypothesize that "discrepancies between aspirations and legitimate chances of achievement increase as one descends in the class structure," and that "the discrepancy between what lower-class youth are led to want and what is actually available to them" is a source of frustration, which may lead them to explore illegal means to achieve culturally approved ends. Cloward and Ohlin take Merton's formulation a step further by distinguishing between legitimate and illegitimate opportunity structures (Merton 1995a; 1997). For some, deviant subcultures, such as those found in criminal organizations, offer alternative, though illicit, structures of opportunity and mobility to those deprived of access to socially approved means of ascent.

How are opportunity structures related to Matthew effects? Merton connects them explicitly in his analysis of opportunities and rewards in science. He observes that the interacting processes of individual self-selection and institutional social selection "affect successive probabilities of access to the opportunity-structure" of a field such as scientific research, and that when the individual's performance meets or exceeds demanding standards of performance, "this initiates *a process of cumulative advantage* in which the individual acquires successively enlarged opportunities to advance his work (and the rewards that go with it) even further" (Merton 1979:89; his italics). Merton acknowledges that other factors apart from individual performance are also at play. This suggests that opportunity structures are like social escalators, providing upward momentum to those who, whether through earned or unearned advantage, manage to reach the lower steps. Presumably, others must use the stairs.

Merton observes that, like individuals, elite research institutions also benefit from the Matthew effect, leveraging their status to accumulate the organizational resources required to attract top-performing scientists. The cumulative advantages of elite scientists and their elite institutions thus feed each other, each contributing to the rising fortunes of the other. Following Merton, we may perhaps speak of micro- and macro-level Matthew effects, the former occurring at the individual level and the latter at the organizational or institutional level, with potential interaction between the two.

We have noted that neither opportunity structures nor access to them is static. Social structures and the individuals who inhabit them are always in flux to some degree. One of the dynamic elements in this flux is the Matthew effect itself. Because such effects are self-amplifying, they introduce an element of change to the systems in which they occur, altering the relative fortunes of social actors and organizations, and thereby expanding or diminishing the opportunities available to them. Whether in science, business, politics, education or everyday life, success tends to lead on to further success, and too often, failure to further failure.

SOCIAL MECHANISMS

The Matthew effect is one example of what Merton calls social mechanisms, defined as "social processes having designated consequences for designated parts of the social structure" (1968c:43). Following Merton and others, Hedström and Swedberg (1998:9) offer a more concrete formulation, represented in the pictograph I → M → O. Social mechanisms (M) transform a system's inputs (I) into outputs (O). The market mechanism in economics is a social mechanism that takes supply and demand inputs and processes them to influence the price and quantity of goods and services available in the marketplace.

Another social mechanism is represented in Merton's (1948) famous analysis of the self-fulfilling prophecy, one of his most celebrated concepts. Merton asks us to imagine that, in 1932, the Last National Bank is fully solvent and doing a thriving business. But on Black Wednesday a false rumor breaks out that the bank is on the verge of bankruptcy. The rumor spreads like an epidemic, and soon crowds of customers are rushing to the bank to withdraw their deposits. As a consequence of this false but self-fulfilling prophecy, the bank fails. In this instance, the rapid diffusion of rumor is the social mechanism that transforms rumors of the bank's financial insolvency into financial ruin, turning a false definition of the situation into a true one.

The logic of the Matthew effect is very similar to the logic of the self-fulfilling prophecy. In each case, an initial condition (I) is amplified by a social mechanism (M), producing an outcome (O) that transforms the initial condition and feeds it back into the system for further amplification. This is what we mean when we say that the

Matthew effect resembles a positive feedback loop. Merton (1968c) hoped that the discovery of social mechanisms would facilitate the development of "theories of the middle range" in sociology, avoiding the extremes of grand abstraction on the one hand and atheoretical research on the other. We revisit the concepts of unintended consequence, opportunity structure, and social mechanism from time to time throughout the course of this book. These and other of Merton's key ideas place our analysis of Matthew effects into the broader context of general social theory.

Merton's own research on cumulative advantage was confined largely to studying reward systems in science. Those who are familiar with his work in the sociology of science may be accustomed to thinking of Matthew effects within this relatively narrow and circumscribed context. But as his collaborator Harriet Zuckerman (1998:155) rightly observes, "the processes associated with cumulative advantage and disadvantage are generic, affecting stratification not just in science but also in other domains of social life," a view that Merton (1988) himself shared. Similarly, DiPrete and Eirich (2006:271) take the expansive view that "cumulative advantage is a general mechanism for inequality across any temporal process (e.g., life course, family generations) in which a favorable relative position becomes a resource that produces further relative gains." Researchers across multiple disciplines in the last several decades have long since brought down the barriers that confined research on cumulative advantage to the sociology of science and have opened up many new lines of inquiry, investigating Matthew effects in virtually every institutional domain. Many sociologists are themselves largely unaware of these emerging developments in other disciplines. This book begins to connect these multiple and often isolated disciplinary studies, joining them into a common discourse.

We have noted that Matthew effects are not all alike, but come in a variety of types. Some Matthew effects are absolute; others are relative. Some may be consciously and intentionally designed into social systems; others arise as unintended consequences of deliberate social action. In Merton's terminology, some are manifest while others remain latent and generally unacknowledged by system participants. Some cumulative advantages may be largely justifiable and deserved, particularly in relatively meritocratic systems, such as scientific research, where they reward extraordinary performance. Others may be largely undeserved, as when they are simply inherited or otherwise received without effort. Finally, Matthew effects may be either positively or negatively functional (or both) for the systems in which they occur.

Because Matthew effects come in so many varieties, they may operate differently in different social contexts. The mechanisms and opportunity structures that we observe in scientific research settings are not identical to those that we observe among school children accumulating vocabulary words, or among entrepreneurs accumulating wealth in the marketplace, or among politicians gerrymandering legislative districts for partisan gain. The reward systems of these respective institutional domains vary considerably. Extraordinary scientific performance is rewarded largely (though not exclusively) in the coin of prestige among colleagues. The principal reward for surpassing academic expectations in school is educational advancement. For the entrepreneur, the primary reward is wealth. For the politician, it is political power. Moreover, the specific performances that are required to secure these rewards vary considerably from one institutional domain to another. Laboratory research, vocabulary acquisition, smart investment, and legislative skill are entirely different activities, with widely varying norms and standards of success. There is virtually no end to the variety of social contexts in which Matthew effects occur.

The concern of this book, however, is less with how the various Matthew effects differ from each other than with what they have in common. What can we say about Matthew effects in general that will allow us to connect the scattered literatures of several disciplines and create a common discourse among them?

Despite their variety, Matthew effects share a defining feature: They all assume the general form of positive feedback loops in systems of stratification. While this book seeks to render Merton's original thinking on Matthew effects faithfully, it also seeks to go a small step beyond Merton, in vocabulary if not in substance, by invoking the phenomenon of positive feedback loops as a recurring feature of cumulative advantage processes, as others have previously suggested (e.g., Allison and Stewart 1974; Allison, Long, and Krauze 1982). Positive feedback loops are said to occur when some part of the output (or consequences) of a system returns to the system as new input and is further amplified, creating a self-perpetuating loop. The accumulation of compound interest is a simple example of such a process. We will have more to say about positive feedback loops in Chapter 3; here it suffices to say that while Merton himself does not rely explicitly on the language of positive feedback in his discussions of cumulative advantage, the concept seems consistent with his analysis. It is through such self-amplifying loops—social mechanisms par excellence—that advantage tends to beget further advantage, expanding structures of opportunity for their beneficiaries and widening the gap between those who have more and those who have less.[7]

We are arguing, in short, for a more expansive usage of the term *Matthew effect* than many sociologists are accustomed to. But that is the point: to expand and extend our awareness of cumulative advantage processes into unexplored realms, as researchers in several disciplines have already begun to do. We are not calling for a new research agenda so much as we are reporting a development in the social sciences that has been occurring for some time. Ours is less a work of new discovery than an attempt at integration and synthesis (Boyer 1990). Without such synthesis, we are left with scattered fragments of research and disconnected discourses.

This book does not argue that the Matthew effect is an iron law of nature or a master principle governing all social and economic outcomes. Clearly, social outcomes are determined by many other factors. Biological, economic, and cultural inheritance; skill, luck, hard work, and initiative; and duplicity and numerous other variables may play a part in determining life's outcomes. In addition, various countervailing forces, to be discussed in Chapter 6, limit cumulative advantage. Furthermore, we do not claim that initial advantages always result in further subsequent advantages. We think in terms of probabilities, not absolute certainties. Initial advantage only tends to beget further advantage, and sometimes it happens that fools—or even smart and hard-working but unlucky investors—and their advantages are soon parted.

The Matthew effect is not, then, the long-awaited universal explanation of everything. In a complex and multicausal world, in which there is reciprocal or circular causation among a multitude of interacting factors (Myrdal 1944; 1957; Stanovich 1986), it is quite unlikely that any such universal principle exists. Single-factor explanations of social phenomena must always to be viewed with extreme skepticism (Myrdal 1944:1069–70).

What we do argue is that Matthew effects are real, found in many different spheres of social life, and potentially powerful determinants of social outcomes in the absence of countervailing factors. By becoming more conscious of these effects in our social systems, we may find more effective ways to counterbalance them when necessary and to neutralize their more pernicious consequences—or, when they are beneficial, to harness them in the service of a common good.

TWO

MATTHEW EFFECTS IN SCIENCE AND TECHNOLOGY

MATTHEW EFFECTS HAVE been observed across a broad spectrum of social institutions, but Merton first developed the concept of cumulative advantage explicitly in the study of scientific institutions. We thus begin by considering some important ways in which advantage tends to beget further advantage in science, as well as in the development and diffusion of technology.

MATTHEW EFFECTS IN SCIENCE

The term *Matthew effect* entered the sociological lexicon in the late 1960s and early 1970s through a series of studies of reward systems in science conducted by scholars affiliated with Columbia University's program in the sociology of science. Robert K. Merton's (1968a) influential essay, "The Matthew Effect in Science," based largely on Harriet Zuckerman's (1972; 1977) subsequently published studies of U.S. Nobel laureates, set off a burst of research (e.g., Cole 1970; Cole and Cole 1973; Zuckerman and Merton 1972) on inequalities in the distribution of scientific rewards.[1] Merton's essay noted the existence of a kind of "class structure" in science, wherein famous scientists have more opportunities than nonfamous scientists to enlarge their reputations. To support this claim, Merton cited Crane's (1965, in Merton 1973:441) earlier finding that "highly productive scientists at a major university gained recognition more often than equally productive scientists at a lesser university." This suggests that even when two scientists are equally productive, the scientist with more prestigious credentials gains more recognition than the scientist with less prestigious credentials. As one Nobel laureate confided, "the man who's best known gets more credit, an inordinate amount of credit" (Merton 1973:443). When two scientists make the same discovery independently, the more famous of the two generally gets the main credit. Thus do the prestigious grow more prestigious.

Merton observed that many Nobel laureates freely acknowledge the disproportionate recognition they receive for collaborations with less-renowned colleagues. Some try to neutralize the Matthew effect by refusing first authorship, or even removing their names entirely from coauthored research to redistribute credit to their fellow scientists (Merton 1973:446; Zuckerman 1968). Here we begin to see that Matthew effects are not inevitable, and can be counteracted though conscious ethical choice. Some Nobel laureates sense a "double injustice" in that famous researchers receive unjust credit while their unknown colleagues are unjustly ignored for work that was genuinely collaborative (Merton 1973:447). As one Nobel laureate in physics put it, "The world is peculiar in this matter of how it gives credit. It tends to give the credit to already famous people" (Zuckerman 1965, discussed in Merton 1988:607). Indeed, it is not unknown for unscrupulous overlings to take credit for work that their less-visible underlings actually produced.

The Matthew effect may produce negative consequences at the individual level, creating a sense of injustice among lesser-known scientists who feel slighted by it. Yet Merton contends that the Matthew effect also may have positive consequences for the system of scientific communication as a whole, especially against the background of overwhelming growth in the volume of scientific literature. A famous name on a scientific paper may be a useful seal of approval, certifying the competence of the work. Furthermore, a well-recognized cadre of elite scientists can be role models for the community, inspiring higher performance among nonelite and future elite scientists. Zuckerman (1977) has found that more than half of Nobel prize–winning scientists have worked under previous Nobel prize winners. While the scientific elite may enjoy excessive personal recognition, Merton argues that their high-profile presence in the scientific community is essential: Their advantaged status indirectly benefits the scientific community as a whole.[2]

Merton concludes that the Matthew effect in science may be viewed as a special case of what he has elsewhere famously called the "self-fulfilling prophecy" (Merton 1948; see Storer 1973:416 on Matthew effects as self-reinforcing). The community's expectation that a famous scientist's latest work will be important leads the community to pay more attention to it, making the scientist even more famous. Younger scientists working with these prominent mentors in prestigious research centers tend to find better jobs and better research connections later on. At the institutional level, this "principle of cumulative advantage" means that centers of scientific excellence receive more resources and prestige, attracting better faculty and students, and thus reinforcing and expanding their initial positions (Merton 1973:457–58). Advantage thus begets further advantage, especially among scientists of exceptional merit who are able, through shrewd and effective use of resources, to turn merely additive advantage into multiplicative advantage (Zuckerman 1998:150–51). At the opposite extreme are those in science or other spheres of life who are wrecked by success, to use Freud's phrase. Unable to manage their fame and fortune wisely, they parlay advantage into disadvantage, proving that Matthew effects are neither inevitable nor eternal.

How strong are Matthew effects in science? Not as strong as we might suppose, according to early studies at Columbia (Cole 1970; Cole and Cole 1973). Scientific institutions are more meritocratic than most, the Coles argue, conferring elite status on those who have clearly demonstrated their merit through excellent performance as judged by universally applied standards. The authors conclude that scientific rewards are largely well deserved, and are not simply the result of advantage attracting further advantage. Similarly, Huber (1998) concludes that the rate of production of patents among inventors seems to have more to do with the giftedness of the inventor than with accumulation of advantage, causing success to breed further success.

Yet even in the relative meritocracy of science, Cole and Cole find some statistical evidence of Matthew effects, confirmed in subsequent research (e.g., Allison, Long, and Krauze 1982; Allison and Stewart 1974). They acknowledge that "scientists gain visibility by publishing significant research. After such visibility is gained, they then enjoy a halo effect [here essentially a Matthew effect] as their research gains additional attention due to their visibility," further widening the gap between elite and average scientists (Cole and Cole 1973:221, 230–31). Statistically analyzing scientific citations, Cole and Cole find that a scientist's reputation and prestige of institutional affiliation both have small independent effects on the reception of the scientist's work: "Lesser papers written by high-ranking scientists are more likely to be widely diffused early than are lesser papers by low-ranking authors" (1973:214; see also 250). As a consequence, "high-ranking scientists are more likely to accumulate citations to their work of relatively small significance," while high-quality papers by low-ranking authors may in rare instances be overlooked entirely (1973:199, 205).[3] Moreover, as two insiders from the world of science observe, "if a paper is written by a group of authors, only one of whom is well known in the field, readers will automatically assume that person is responsible. A paper signed by Nobody, Nobody, and Somebody will be casually referred to as 'work done in Somebody's lab,' and even sometimes cited (incorrectly) in the literature as due to 'Somebody, et al.'" (Goodstein and Woodward 1999:88).

Matthew effects in science may also arise through invisible colleges (Crane 1972), social networks of scientists whose members regularly communicate with each other, often publish together, and tend to cite each other's work. Members of invisible colleges may thereby promote each other's visibility and professional success at the expense of scientists who are less well-connected (Blashfield, Guze, Strauss, Katz, and Kendell 1982).

Various strategies have been proposed to reduce unfair Matthew effects in science. It is sometimes alleged that scientific journals accept or reject a paper based on the prestige of the author's institutional affiliation rather than on the paper's own merits, enabling the prestigious to become more prestigious. To guard against this possibility, many journals have instituted a blind reviewing process in which the author's identity and affiliation are concealed from the manuscript reviewer, an editorial practice that has both its critics and defenders (Garfunkel, Ulshen, Hamrick, and Lawson 1994).

Issues of fairness are also raised by those who contend that Matthew effects perpetuate sex discrimination in science. It is beyond dispute that women historically have been discouraged, and even systematically prohibited, from pursuing scientific careers (Rossiter 1993; 1995; Cole 1979; Zuckerman, Cole, and Bruer 1991). The presumption that science is a "man's world" is so pervasive that even as recently as the 1970s, scientists were still routinely referred to as "men of science," as though women scientists did not exist. While Matthew effects may or may not have affected particular instances of alleged sex discrimination,[4] there can be little doubt that scientific disciplines in general have historically favored men over women, and that male advantages have often been self-perpetuating.

Science historian Margaret Rossiter (1993; 1995) has proposed the existence of a "Matilda effect"—a Matthew effect in science that has historically promoted cumulative male advantage and female disadvantage through the operation of old-boy networks and other discriminatory practices. Subsequent research (e.g., Sonnert and Holton 1995) confirms Rossiter's claims. Clark and Corcoran (1986) find that the stages of women's academic careers, from recruitment to entry to career persistence, may be undermined by gender-specific obstacles and lack of social supports. Valian (1999) has made Matthew effects central to her analysis of why women have not advanced more rapidly in science and other professions. She draws on several previous studies of the effects of accumulated advantage and disadvantage (e.g., Cole 1979; Cole and Singer 1991; Fox 1981; 1985; Long 1990; 1992; Merton 1968a; Zuckerman 1987) to demonstrate how small initial differences in the evaluation of performance can accumulate to create large gender differences in salary, promotion, and prestige. Gender discrimination in science has been the subject of lively controversy following a much publicized statement by former Harvard University president Lawrence Summers attributing women's underrepresentation in the sciences primarily to biological rather than to social factors

(Fogg 2005). Summers later recanted his statement, acknowledging that gender discrimination is still a significant issue in the world of science.

If Matthew effects are observed in scientific institutions, where rewards are based largely on well-defined standards of merit, they may be even more prevalent in systems that are less highly codified, and in which criteria for success are more ambiguous, as Zuckerman and Merton (1972:507) seem to suggest. Matthew effects may be stronger in the world of art than in the world of science. Insofar as the quality of an artist's work is difficult or impossible to quantify, idiosyncratic (if not arbitrary) social judgments may be crucial in determining the artist's status. A favorable judgment by a well-placed critic may echo through the halls of the art community and beyond, helping the artist to become famous for being famous.

In academia, Matthew effects are not confined to the sciences, but may be found across many disciplines. In the field of management, Hunt and Blair (1987) propose that Matthew effects reward not only those who make high-profile contributions to scholarship in their field, but also, though to a lesser degree, those who become well known by contributing to their disciplines in more indirect ways, such as by serving in the offices and committees of the discipline's professional associations. Both direct and indirect contributions to one's field increase one's professional recognition and advantage; these may, in turn, attract further resources, leading to still further recognition.

We observe Matthew effects in academia not only at the micro-level of the individual, but at the macro-level of institutions as well (Merton 1968a; 1988). Hanish, Horan, Keen, St. Peter, Ceperich, and Beasley (1995) have challenged the influence of Matthew effects in rating graduate programs in psychology. The authors criticize rating methodologies based less on demonstrable scholarly productivity—measured, for instance, by the frequency of scholarly citations to the work of faculties—than on prestigious institutional reputations that current performance may or may not justify. Reputational rankings, they argue, set into motion a self-perpetuating cycle, in which traditionally prestigious institutions continue to reap windfall profits of underserved recognition.

At an even more macro-level, Matthew effects have been observed in the global organization of science. Bonitz (1997; 2002; 2005) and his colleagues in Germany examine a Matthew effect for countries (MEC), which occurs when wealthy nations—particularly North American and European countries—with well-established and well-funded scientific facilities and personnel receive more than their statistically expected share of citations in leading scientific journals while less-developed countries receive lesser shares.

Closely related to this phenomenon is brain drain, or the recruitment and development of scientific and other educated talent, usually though not always from less- to more-developed countries. This tends to benefit the latter at the expense of the former (Cervantes and Guellec 2002). Brain drains have been described as a kind of human capital flight: Like the flight of financial capital from less to more advantaged countries, they drain much-needed resources from poorer nations and hinder their development. Brain drains thus tend to reinforce the power and privilege of nations at the center of the world system while stifling efforts among nations on the periphery to escape dependency (Schott 1998).

MATTHEW EFFECTS IN TECHNOLOGY

Matthew effects arise not only in science and academia generally, but also in the rapidly changing world of technology. New technologies build upon previous technologies, and thus, as Diamond (1997:258) succinctly puts it, "technology begets more technology." The history of technology offers numerous examples of this "autocatalytic process: that is, one that speeds up at a rate that increases with time, because the process catalyzes itself."[5] For Diamond, autocatalytic processes have set off technological explosions of innovation at pivotal times throughout human history, including periods of rapid innovation during the Bronze Age, the later Middle Ages, and our own time. Similarly, Lenski and Lenski (1970:82–83) observe that new inventions are frequently recombinations of existing inventions. Thus, the greater the number of inventions that currently exist, the greater the number of possible new inventions. Each new invention increases the possibility of further invention.

Autocatalytic processes may help us to understand the current rapid rates of innovation in the field of information technology. Consider the Microsoft Corporation's meteoric rise to competitive dominance in the software industry beginning in the 1980s (Freiberger and Swaine 2000). Microsoft's operating system, MS-DOS, marketed in collaboration with IBM, secured the young company's initial advantage in the personal computer market. The financial success of this initial product paved the way for research and development of subsequent products, most notably, the Windows operating systems. As Windows gained widespread popularity, it became a vehicle for bundling and selling other Microsoft products, producing revenue for still further research and development. Technological advantage begot further advantage and the rich got richer. At the same time, Microsoft's word processing program, Word, gained market momentum against competing products through a positive feedback process similar to the Matthew effect, which economists call "increasing returns" (Arthur 1990; 1996). Increasing returns occur when a product gains value with every additional unit produced. One telephone is of no use, for example, unless there are other telephones with which to network, and the more the better. Many information technologies, including word processing, appear to be governed by the economics of increasing returns. New users of Word sought compatibility with current users in the belief that everyone was using it, and a positive feedback loop was set into motion—a classic instance of the principle that the more you sell, the more you sell. Word, like Windows, became the industry standard, and Microsoft founder Bill Gates became the world's richest person, carried aloft, in large part, by the powerful momentum of the Matthew effect.

Meanwhile, an emerging digital divide between those who had access to information technology and those who did not—that is, the divide between richer and poorer, white and black, male and female, affluent urban-suburban and rural—grew wider during the 1990s (NTIA 1999). As Levesque (2000:2) observes, the technologically rich got richer while the technologically poor fell further behind, at least in relative terms.

By the century's end, however, the digital divide appeared to narrow as information technology became less expensive and more widely available, making computers more accessible to disadvantaged segments of the population (Pew Charitable Trusts 2007; Samuelson 2002b;). While the digital divide may now be closing among individuals and groups within the United States, it may be widening at the global level as the economic gap between the richest and poorest nations continues to grow. Advanced industrial countries, such as the United States, as well as rising economic powers, such as China and India, continue to progress at breakneck speed on the technological front, leaving those in the least-developed countries, especially in Africa, further behind. Ishaq (2001) reports that nearly 54 percent of the population in the United States and Canada were Internet users in November 2000, compared with 14 percent in Europe, 3 percent in Latin America, 1 percent in the Middle East, and fewer than 1 percent in Africa. Ishaq emphasizes that connectivity will be essential to the future of developing regions, not only in commercial development, but in governmental, agricultural, educational, and medical development as well. He and many others are therefore concerned by the prospect of a growing global digital divide.

If we think of international technological advantage in terms of population percentages—that is, the percentages of a population using telephones, watching television, or accessing the Internet—we may speak of a ceiling of universal usage for particular technologies. Those in the most developed countries may eventually reach a limit to Internet usage as they approach universal connectivity and market saturation. Less-developed countries, on the other hand, have nowhere to go but up in their access to information technology, and may thus begin to close the digital gap in future years, if only because their usage rates have more room to grow.

However, we do not know the upper limit of technological complexity and sophistication because research and development are continually pushing that limit upward. Seen in this way, there may be virtually no limit to the size of the technological gap that could continue to grow between rich and poor nations, just as there is no known upper limit to the size of the economic gap that is now widening between the world's richest and poorest nations. It is to these economic inequalities that we now turn our attention.

THREE

MATTHEW EFFECTS IN THE ECONOMY

EARLY RESEARCH ON Matthew effects focused on in-equalities in the reward systems of science. Norman Storer (1973:416), affiliated with Columbia University's sociology of science program, was among the first to state explicitly that such effects might be discovered in other social institutions as well, including economic systems. There are obviously important differences between scientific and economic institutions.[1] Yet despite their differences, we may observe Matthew effects in both domains. This chapter identifies instances in which self-amplifying (or deamplifying) processes occur in economic systems. It is beyond the scope of this book to analyze each instance in detail. Rather, the chapter offers a broad array of illustrative examples of such processes in the economic sphere, conveying a sense of the prevalence of self-amplifying processes in economic life. The focus throughout is on how positive feedback loops can operate to the advantage of those who are already advantaged to begin with.

This chapter is not about how economists think about inequality and its sources. Economists rarely refer to the Matthew effect by that name and they seem largely unaware of the large literature that has grown up around the concept in other disciplines. We have more to say about how economists think about inequality in the appendix, where we examine national and world trends in economic inequality. Economists rightly attribute inequalities to a multitude of complex factors, and Matthew effects are only one factor among many others that help to explain disparities in the distribution of resources. As we have noted, the Matthew effect is not an iron law of nature; it operates in a world of relative probabilities, not absolute certainties. In a complex world, the rich do not always get richer, nor the poor poorer. We claim only that, other things equal, advantage tends to beget further advantage and disadvantage further disadvantage. But other things are never equal, and many other factors may countervail these tendencies, as we will discuss in Chapter 6. Countervailing factors that may limit or mute Matthew effects include statistical phenomena, such as floor and ceiling effects; intergenerational dispersion of wealth; the vicissitudes of competition in a market economy; egalitarian social movements, such as the labor and civil rights movements; government intervention, such as progressive and estate taxation; and altruistic or enlightened self-interested behavior, as exemplified by the well-known philanthropy of Bill Gates and Warren Buffett. We applaud these countervailing forces when they restrain the more pernicious effects of inequality. This book makes no pretense to being neutral with regard to extreme inequalities: Our view stands in a moral tradition that considers extreme inequalities as destructive of human well-being and inimical to the common good.

Although economists rarely refer to the Matthew effect by that name, the essential principle that advantage begets further advantage is well known in economic thought. An absolute Matthew effect is implied, for example, in Marx and Engels' (1955 [1848]) and Marx's (1967 [1867]) accounts of the accumulation and concentration of capital in the hands of an increasingly dominant capitalist class at the expense of an increasingly impoverished proletariat in nineteenth-century Europe. Marx depicted a system in which capitalists confiscate the fruits of their workers' labor and reinvest the profits to accumulate still more wealth. In systems based on exploitation, the rich do not merely get rich while the poor get poorer; they get richer because the poor get poorer. Marx's analysis, however flawed it may be in retrospect, points to the need to distinguish between exploitative and nonexploitative Matthew effects. In the former, the gains of the advantaged are won at the expense of the disadvantaged—a condition known in game theory as a zero-sum game, wherein one player's gain is another's loss. Positive-sum games, by contrast, are potentially less exploitive, as all players may benefit, though some may benefit considerably more than others.

A rather different notion of cumulative advantage is implied in Max Weber's (1958 [1905]) classic account of the Protestant work ethic and the rise of modern capitalism. According to Weber, devout Calvinists in eighteenth-century Europe were motivated by religious conviction to work hard and prosper. But because their ascetic beliefs forbade them to spend their profits on worldly pleasures, they reinvested these profits to expand their business enterprises. The resulting accumulation and amplification of capital fueled further economic growth, propelling what economic development theorist W.W. Rostow (1960; 1980) would later call an "economic take-off." Thus Weber attributed the rise of modern capitalism, in part, to a kind of Matthew effect. While Weber's thesis has been widely criticized, it has also had its champions (e.g., Landes 1998; McClelland 1961) among those who invoke the work ethic as an important cultural factor in the accumulation of capital and the dynamics of modernization. Weber's account of the rise of capitalism is quite different from Marx's, but both identify a self-amplifying feedback loop, as we now call it, as an important social and economic mechanism underlying capital accumulation.

ECONOMIC MATTHEW MECHANISMS

It is well known in the business world that advantage begets further advantage. Several clichés of commerce reflect this awareness: "It takes money to make money." "The big fish eat the little fish." "Success breeds success." "Big dogs eat first." "The first million is the hardest."[2] Each of these popular sayings candidly acknowledges that those who enjoy initial advantages in business are well positioned to parlay these advantages into further advantages. Consider several social mechanisms that tend to favor the advantaged over the disadvantaged in the everyday workings of the economy. In each instance, positive feedback loops amplify initial advantage—a signature characteristic of Matthew effects.

INHERITED ADVANTAGE

First there is the mechanism of inherited advantage. Through the luck of the birth lottery, some are born into advantage and others into disadvantage. Mark Twain's ironic remark that he chose his parents wisely reminds us that we do not control the time, place, or social circumstances of our births. Some are born with relatively easy access to opportunity structures, others begin life with almost no access, and still others—most of us—fall between the extremes. But whether we are born rich, poor, or in between, we are all subject to the luck of the lottery, and the social locations of our births substantially influence our subsequent life chances.

To vary the gambling metaphor, we do not choose the cards we are dealt in life, though we have some control over how we play them. Niccolo Machiavelli (1981 [1532]) observed that life's outcomes are a combination of *fortuna,* circumstances beyond our control, and *virtu,* our skills and abilities. *Fortuna* is the hand of cards we are dealt, while *virtu* is the skill with which we play them. Machiavelli contended that *fortuna* and *virtu* determine life's outcomes in roughly equal measure.

In American culture, we often seem to exaggerate the role of *virtu* and to understate the role of *fortuna* in determining life's outcomes. Many still embrace the cultural myth of the self-made man, as though any of us could create ourselves in a social vacuum. The advantages or disadvantages we inherit—not only our economic circumstances, but our genetic, family, and cultural circumstances as well—all shape who we later become. The child born to an impoverished mother in a remote village of Somalia, or even a rough neighborhood in an American city, does not enjoy the same life chances as a child born to comfort and security. Some find ways to overcome their initial disadvantages, or to squander their advantages, but there is no doubt that those who begin life with large advantages enjoy a higher probability of success than those who do not. And as we have previously seen, Matthew effects can turn even small initial advantages into large gains.

COMPOUND INTEREST AND RETURN
ON INVESTMENT

In Chapter 1 we compared the operation of Matthew effects to the accumulation of compound interest. Valian (1999:3), in a study of gender inequalities, notes that "like interest on capital, advantages accrue, and that, like interest on debt, disadvantages also accumulate. Very small differences . . . as they pile up, result in large disparities."

In the simple mathematics of compound interest, if we deposit money in the bank at a given rate of interest and then return this interest to the existing principal, our money does not grow in a simple linear fashion. Rather, the interest added to principal accumulates still more interest through a positive feedback mechanism, causing the principal to grow at an accelerating rate through time—that is, exponentially.

Because compound interest grows exponentially, it benefits above all those who begin with a larger initial principal. The sayings in business that "it takes money to make money" and that "the first million is the hardest" reflect the recognition that those who begin with the greatest advantages are positioned to make the greatest gains. As we saw in Chapter 1, even when the compounded return on investment of a large and a small depositor grow at the same rate, the mathematics of compound interest ensures that the dollar gap between the two widens progressively over time, creating a relative Matthew effect. The result of such inequalities in initial bargaining power is a widening disparity in the subsequent fortunes of the more and less advantaged.

There is also often an absolute (and not merely a relative) Matthew effect in the relationship between lender and debtor. Not uncommonly, the lender grows richer as the debtor grows poorer. Anyone who has ever taken out a mortgage knows that the interest on a loan can equal or exceed the principal, enriching the bank while draining the borrower. This is especially true of the poor, who, if they do not qualify for loans from established institutions, may turn instead to usurious lenders charging exorbitant rates of interest. There is some evidence that the poor often pay more for the same goods and services in general, and especially for loans (Oliver and Shapiro 2006:223; Squires 2004). Thus, many are caught in downward financial spirals from which they may never recover, dragged beneath the financial waves by the undertow of compounded debt.

Whether through inheritance, investment, or work, some enjoy vastly more accumulated assets than others. In the United States, wealth is far more unevenly distributed than income. Caner and Wolff (2004) demonstrate that poverty rates would be much higher if poverty were measured not by income, but by accumulated assets. They find that racial and ethnic minorities and those with less education lag far behind whites and those with more education in average net worth: The average net worth of African-American and Hispanic households in the United States is only about one-tenth that of white non-Hispanic households (Kochhar 2004; Oliver and Shapiro 1995; 2006; Shapiro 2004). And while many federal policies promote asset building, such as tax subsidies for home ownership, retirement accounts, reductions in capital gains and inheritance tax rates, and budgetary outlays that benefit small businesses, most of these policies disproportionately benefit those who already hold substantial assets and do little to help those in poverty to create better financial futures for themselves (Woo, Schweke, and Buchholz 2004). Such federal policies thus help the most advantaged to amplify their advantages and pass these on to future generations.

PROMOTION AND COMPENSATION PRACTICES

Positive feedback loops are also evident in the promotion and compensation practices of organizations. As noted in Chapter 2, small initial differences in the evaluation of employee performance can have dramatic long-term consequences for promotion and salary. In a computer simulation, Martell, Lane, and Emrich (1996; discussed in Valian 1999:3) created an organization with an eight-level hierarchy, in which a small (1 percent) pro-male bias in promotions, operating on a population composed equally of men and women at the bottom level, eventually resulted in an executive stratum composed of 65 percent males at the highest level of the hierarchy. This tendency for small initial differences to produce large subsequent differences resembles the famous butterfly effect discovered in the emerging branch of science known as chaos theory (Gleick 1987:8), which hypothesizes that the flutter of a butterfly's wing in Beijing, continuously amplified, could create a storm system over New York.

Matthew effects are also evident in the salary policies of organizations. Consider the practice of assigning wage and salary increases based on across-the-board percentages. Suppose that a secretary making $20,000 per year and an executive making $200,000 both receive a 5 percent salary increase for three successive years. While they receive an equal rate of increase, the secretary's salary over three years has increased in amount to only $23,153, a raise of $3,153. The executive's salary, meanwhile, has grown to $231,525, a raise of $31,153. The executive's raise is now larger than the secretary's entire salary as the dollar gap between them widens rapidly. As both receive the same rate of increase in salary, some may consider the compensation to be fair. But people do not spend rates; they spend money. From this perspective, the secretary is falling ever farther behind.

Conventional economic measures of inequality, such as the Gini coefficient, do not interpret the widening income gap between secretary and boss as an instance of growing inequality, as the ratio of their salaries remains the same and does not alter their respective shares of income. Alternative methods of measuring economic equality are discussed in the appendix; let it suffice here to say that the widening financial disparity between secretary and boss, like the widening disparities produced by compound interest at varying levels of initial principal, is an instance of what Firebaugh (2003:73) has called "gap inequality." This form of inequality, while not registered in measures such as the Gini coefficient, is nonetheless important to acknowledge. Mechanisms such as compound interest and similar processes that produce widening disparities, are obviously not the only factors involved in generating inequalities, but they are nonetheless an indispensable piece of the larger puzzle.

Widening inequalities between those at the top of the economic ladder and those at the bottom create a society of extreme contrasts. At one extreme are those who work at menial jobs for minimum wage or less—those who are being "nickeled and dimed" to death, in Barbara Ehrenreich's (2001) vivid phrase—and whose lives are a constant struggle merely to survive. At the other extreme are those whose levels of compensation are almost beyond comprehension, in what Frank and Cook (1996) have called the winner-take-all society. The authors argue that an elite stratum of corporate executives, athletes, entertainers, and others now compete nationally and internationally in winner-take-all markets, or more accurately, markets in which those at the top receive a grossly disproportionate share of rewards in a "world increasingly unrestrained by inhibitions about greed" (1999:3, 5). Frank and Cook contend that such markets do not necessarily serve the public interest. In sports and entertainment, very small differences in performance may result in disproportionately large differences in reward, with commensurate increases in ticket prices at the stadium or concert venue. Rosen (1981) sheds further light on the economics of superstars when he observes that communication technologies, such as television, CDs, and DVDs, have generally diminished the price of entertainment services, but vastly expanded the size of audiences who may enjoy the superstars' performances, thus greatly enhancing the salaries that such performers can command.

Regarding executive compensation, Frank and Cook cite Graef's (1991) estimates that in 1974, chief executive officers (CEOs) of large American corporations were compensated at 35 times the rate of average manufacturing workers. By the 1990s, that ratio had risen to 120, with many top CEOs earning more than $10 million a year. By 2000, the CEO-to-average worker ratio had reached 525 to 1 (AFL-CIO 2008), and *The Economist* (2003:8) reported that among *Fortune* magazine's top 100 corporations, chief executive compensation had reached 1,000 times the level for ordinary workers, though these ratios have subsequently declined in the face of increasing public scrutiny and criticism (AFL-CIO 2008). Frank and Cook contend that such astronomical levels of compensation make little economic sense and come directly out of the pockets of shareholders—or, one might add, out of the pockets of employees, whose own earnings stagnated or declined in real terms while executive salaries and benefits skyrocketed.

Winner-take-all markets have set into motion what Frank and Cook describe as arms races, in which elite salaries are bid skyward in a frenzy of unregulated competition. In response to such arms races, professional sports leagues have instituted a variety of arms-control agreements, ranging from roster limits and salary caps to revenue-sharing plans and restrictions on free agency (1996:168–71) in an attempt to restrain these bidding wars. The authors note that similar arms races, and attempts to head them off, are increasingly evident among corporate executives and their stockholders.

BARGAINING ADVANTAGES

Matthew effects also occur in bargaining processes in which those in advantaged positions can extract favorable terms from those who come to the table with less. Imagine the case of a person with few financial or educational advantages who is looking for a job to feed his or her family. Elster (1982:474, 474n) notes that for a bargainer with few resources,

> even a small gain is so important that he can be made to be content with it, whereas the more affluent can say with equanimity, "Take it or leave it." The Matthew effect may itself be seen as a form of exploitation, or at least as contrary to distributive justice, which rather demands that the least advantaged person should be given more. . . . Perhaps Marx had something like this in mind when he wrote [in *Theories of Surplus Value*] that in some forms of international trade, the "richer country exploits the poorer one, even when the latter gains by the exchange."

Matthew effects may occur, in short, when bargaining occurs between asymmetric partners (Veugelers and Kesteloot 1996). With the decline of trade unions due to international wage competition and other factors, vulnerable employees are increasingly at a bargaining disadvantage with their employers, who can afford to say "take it or leave it."

ECONOMIES OF SCALE

Matthew effects also play a role in the strategies of large corporations as they seek to drive their smaller competitors out of business. Large corporations enjoy cost advantages made possible by economies of scale: Their sheer size and resources typically allow them to produce or purchase goods at a lower unit cost than their smaller competitors, pushing competitors out of business and taking over their share of the market. Large retail chains, such as WalMart, have become targets of protest in recent years for driving local businesses to extinction, eliminating family-owned stores in cities and small towns across America. Corporations with vast resources can often afford to undersell their competitors, even at a loss if necessary, until competitors with fewer resources go under, allowing the victors to raise prices again. This practice, which economists call predatory pricing or dumping, helps big fish to eat little fish in the icy waters of commerce.

MONOPOLY, OLIGOPOLY, AND MARKET COMPETITION

Wherever we find large concentrations of wealth and economic power, unchecked by law or economic competition, we are liable to find processes of cumulative advantage. In the absence of effective governmental antitrust regulation and vigorous price competition in the marketplace, monopolies and oligopolistic cartels may inflate profits by raising prices through practices such as price fixing and price gouging.

The economic concept of increasing returns (Arthur 1990; 1996) sheds light on how monopolies and oligopolies form in an age of high technology. As noted in Chapter 2, increasing returns occur when the value of a product increases with its number of users. The telephone becomes a more valuable technology as its network of users expands. Firms such as Microsoft, Amazon, eBay, and Google have benefited from such returns and dominated their markets in recent years as new users have rushed to adopt what they perceive others to be using. More users beget still more users. Thus increasing returns act as positive feedback loops to produce Matthew effects in the corporate world.

Marketers have long been aware of the power of such positive feedback loops to move products and capture markets. Shermer (2007:iv) has invoked the Matthew effect (which he also calls the best-seller effect) to explain the self-amplifying cycle whereby prominent marketing displays trigger increased sales, which result in further publicity, stimulating further sales. Shermer (2008) also observes Matthew effects in the political marketplace, where candidates, as competing products, vie for market dominance. He remarks that "polls and media coverage confer the Matthew Effect upon certain candidates, thereby shifting voter preferences and loyalties like so many brands in the supermarket [and] creating a positive feedback loop in which the media-rich candidate [becomes] even richer"—a phenomenon better known in political science as the bandwagon effect. Cultural fads and fashions have been seen to spread in a similar nonlinear fashion, reaching tipping points (Gladwell 2000) at which the rate of growth in the adoption of a new product or practice suddenly accelerates dramatically.

FLAT AND REGRESSIVE TAXES

Still another economic sphere in which Matthew effects operate is taxation. Chapter 4 examines the impact of progressive, regressive, and flat tax-rate structures on inequality. Regressive taxes and tax cuts that benefit primarily upper income groups have the effect, at least in the short term, of redistributing wealth and income upward, creating a widening gap between upper and lower income groups and creating relative, if not absolute, Matthew effects. In principle, progressive federal and state income taxes, which tax higher incomes at higher rates, are designed to have the opposite effect, redistributing advantages to middle and lower income groups. In practice, however, accountants and attorneys skilled in the arts of legal tax avoidance (if not tax evasion) can significantly undermine the egalitarian effects of progressive taxation.

◉ ◉ ◉

These are among the mechanisms that tend to promote widening economic inequalities, and each of these mechanisms involves a circular and self-amplifying causal loop. In the case of compound interest, new interest is returned to principal, generating further interest. In employee compensation, salary increases become a part of the base upon which future salary increases are calculated. In bargaining advantage and economies of scale, the sheer size and strength of dominant actors permit them to take advantage of the weaknesses of subordinates or competitors. In each instance, initial advantages are amplified, creating a widening gap between the more advantaged and the less advantaged.

This principle of circular and cumulative causation was developed by the Swedish Nobel prize–winning economist Gunnar Myrdal (1939; 1944; 1957; 1970) several years before Merton coined the term *Matthew effect*. Myrdal's principle is so closely related to Merton's, and so essential to its understanding, that we now examine it more closely.

CIRCULAR CAUSATION AND THE MATTHEW EFFECT: MYRDAL MEETS MERTON

In *An American Dilemma* (1944), Myrdal's classic study of race relations in the United States, he observed a vicious circle in relations between blacks and whites. He contended that "White prejudice and discrimination keep the Negro low in standards of living, health, education, manners and morals. This, in turn, gives support to white prejudice. White prejudice and Negro standards thus mutually 'cause' each other" (1944:75). If either of these factors changes, the other also changes. If white prejudice and discrimination intensify, Myrdal hypothesized, we should observe a vicious circle spiraling downward, as further deterioration of living standards among blacks leads to still further prejudice and discrimination among whites. On the other hand, any amelioration of white prejudice and discrimination, or of black living standards, should influence the other in a positive direction, setting into motion a virtuous circle leading to improved relations between races. Myrdal's analysis here is strikingly similar to

Merton's (1948) analysis of race relations in his essay on the self-ful-filling prophecy.

In later works, Myrdal applied the principle of circular causation to the study of world poverty (1957; 1970), viewing poverty as a vicious circle that is at once both a cause and an effect. In the words of Rag-nar Nurske (quoted in Myrdal 1944:11–12), "a poor man may not have enough to eat; being undernourished, his health may be weak; being physically weak, his working capacity may be low, which means that he is poor, which in turn means that he will not have enough to eat, and so on." The same vicious circle, Myrdal argued, applies on a larger scale to poor countries as a whole, which too often fall farther and farther behind rich countries in the struggle for economic advantage. Myrdal sought ways to break such vicious circles of poverty and to supplant them with virtuous circles. "Quite obviously," he observed, "a circular relationship between less poverty, more food, improved health and higher working capacity would sustain a cumulative pro-cess upward rather than downward."

Economists have discerned a variety of other causal circles that snare people in poverty traps. Banerjee and Mullainathan (2008) have examined the circular relation between poverty and local productiv-ity. They argue that the affluent enjoy a self-amplifying advantage over the poor in productivity and income insofar as the affluent can afford to subcontract domestic tasks that would otherwise demand their at-tention, freeing them to dedicate their time and energy more fully to economically productive activity. The poor, however, are commonly distracted by issues of sheer domestic survival that sap their attention, time, and energy, thereby diminishing their productivity at work.

The vicious cycles of poverty that Myrdal describes are observed in developed as well as developing countries. Social critics such as Ehren-reich (2001) and Shipler (2005) have a gift for putting a human face on the self-sustaining dynamics of poverty. Shipler recounts the story of Caroline: "The people who got promotions tended to have something that Caroline did not. They had teeth." Caroline had lost her teeth because she could not afford proper dental care. Shipler (2005:52–53) observes that if "she had not been poor, she would not have lost her teeth, and if she had not lost her teeth, perhaps she would not have remained poor." Lack of proper health care and nutrition, educational credentials, means of transportation, socially approved dress and appearance, and social or linguistic skills can all be formidable impediments to escaping from poverty.

The vicious downward spirals that Myrdal describes strikingly resemble Merton's Matthew effects.[3] On at least three occasions (1957:12, 34; 1970:281), Myrdal even quotes the same verses from the Gospel of Matthew that Merton cites. Myrdal finds in these scriptures evidence of an ancient "understanding of the fact, which in our analysis will be given much importance, namely that the cumulative process, if not regulated, will cause increasing inequalities" (1957:12; see also 1970:281).[4]

Merton's Matthew effect and Myrdal's circular causation both illustrate how feedback loops in social systems operate. Let us look at these processes more closely. In the language of cybernetics and systems theory, feedback is a circular causal process in which some part of a system's output reenters the system as new input. As noted in Chapter 1, systems theorists distinguish between negative and positive feedback loops. Negative feedback loops generally stabilize a system by reducing deviations from some desired goal-state or state of equilibrium. A familiar mechanical example is the thermostat (Wiener 1961:97). When a room grows too hot or too cold, the thermostat detects deviations from a desired temperature and activates the heater or air conditioner to bring the room back to the desired setpoint. Output from the heating and cooling system is fed back into the system as information, allowing the system to compare actual and desired temperature and thus to effectively regulate the indoor climate. Homeostatic processes that regulate the body's temperature and other internal states are also often described as negative feedback mechanisms, though some theorists (e.g., Buckley 1967:53; Scott 1995:144–55) insist that the term *feedback* be reserved exclusively for systems guided by conscious purposes and goals.

Positive feedback loops, by contrast, amplify deviations from some desired goal-state, thus tending to destabilize systems. A familiar example of positive feedback is the screech that we hear from a sound system when sound signals, entering a microphone and amplified through a nearby loudspeaker, return to the microphone to be amplified again and again in a vicious circle. Such events usually represent a failure of regulation within a system. Matthew effects resemble positive feedback loops insofar as they tend, in the absence of intervention, to produce self-amplifying cycles of inequality that may threaten to undermine the stability of social systems.

A clear example of a positive feedback loop operating in a social system is the population explosion. Suppose that a country desires to stabilize its population size. If the population of reproducing adults produces more children than are needed to maintain a desired population size, most of these children later reenter the reproduction system as adults, producing still more children and contributing to a vicious circle of overpopulation. Without effective intervention, such as family planning and birth-control policies, population growth tends to spin out of control.

Matthew effects and causal circles are essential to understanding the dynamics of inequality not only among individuals, but among communities and societies as well. Myrdal boldly asserts that "circular causation has validity over the entire field of social relations. It should be the main hypothesis when studying economic underdevelopment and development" (1957:23). Myrdal offers the following illustration of the principle at a local level.

Imagine that a factory in a community, employing a large part of the population, burns down and is not rebuilt. The firm owning the factory goes out of business and its workers become unemployed. This sets into motion a vicious circle. Decreasing income leads to decreasing demand, causing other businesses in the community to lose income and lay off workers. The further loss of income and demand makes the community less attractive to outside businesses and workers who may have otherwise considered moving in. As the vicious circle accelerates, residents move out to seek better opportunities elsewhere. A shrinking tax base leads the municipal government to raise tax rates or cut services and school funding, making the community still less attractive to outsiders and causing more residents to leave.

Disadvantage begets further disadvantage, and the community slides more deeply into decline (1957:23–34). The effects are circular and cumulative, creating a downward spiral.

Let us now imagine a second community with a happier fate. A new industry moves in, creating opportunities for employment and higher incomes. Local businesses flourish as income and demand increase. The dynamism of the local economy attracts additional new businesses and investment, leading to enhanced tax revenue and improved public services. Advantage begets further advantage, setting into motion an upward spiral (1957:25–26). Economist Paul Krugman (2001) offers this real-life example: "What keeps New York a great city is circular causation; people and businesses locate there because of the opportunities created by the presence of other people and businesses."

Finally—and here we extend Myrdal's parable in ways that are consistent with his subsequent analysis—imagine that the fates of these two communities are interlocked. Suppose the first community's factory did not burn down, but that its owners simply relocated production to the second community, setting into motion a downward spiral in the former locale and an upward spiral in the latter. Myrdal insists that the dynamics of cumulative causation, whether at the local, national, or international level, favor some communities, regions, or nations at the expense of others. One economy's upward spiral may be an important cause of another's downward spiral. Concretely, we observe such spirals in the movement of industries from declining rust-belt communities in the United States to growing sun-belt communities and Mexican border cities, or more recently, from regions of Mexico to regions of China.

Myrdal argued that the play of the free market without intervention tends to increase inequalities within and among nations. Market forces tend to attract and concentrate capital, skilled labor, and other resources in favored central locales, creating backwash effects—that is, negative consequences for the less advantaged—in peripheral areas. Prosperous centers of economic activity extract profits, talent, raw materials, and other resources from the hinterlands, causing the latter regions to fall farther behind. The process is circular and cumulative as resources attract further resources in a circle of growth at the center and decline at the edge. Rich regions of a country grow richer as poor regions grow poorer.

Of course, not all benefits of economic growth flow from peripheries to centers. Some portion of a center's prosperity trickles downward or outward to its periphery. A thriving center may create increasing demand for agricultural products from the periphery, or new jobs for miners. But these spread effects—that is, positive consequences for the less advantaged—that flow from richer to poorer regions do not necessarily result in greater equality between center and periphery. Myrdal contended that, on balance, backwash effects exceed spread effects, at least in the less-developed world. The center takes more from the periphery than it gives back. The centripetal forces of economic concentration typically overpower the centrifugal forces of spread benefits, resulting in widening inequalities between center and periphery. Thus, peripheral regions tend to stagnate and decline as economic centers flourish (1957:27–32). Moreover, "this tendency becomes the more dominant, the poorer a country is" (1957:34–35). Myrdal saw this dynamic occurring not just within or among the regions of a country, but also among countries, creating economic inequalities and moral inequities on an international scale.

So far, we have examined Myrdal's focus on the play of market forces under laissez-faire regulations, a condition that he expects to generate inequalities. Can the state, by pursuing more just and egalitarian policies, moderate the inequities of the market system? Can state policy offset backwash effects and strengthen spread effects within or among regions? Myrdal responds by affirming the value of democratic and egalitarian public policy. He observes that, in practice, concentrations of economic power in underdeveloped countries are linked to undemocratic concentrations of political power. This sets up a vicious circle of causation between the economy and the state, through which economic elites control quasi-feudal political institutions and exercise governmental power in ways that further expand their economic advantages. By contrast, more economically developed societies enjoy relatively more democratic and egalitarian political systems, limiting the power of economic elites to control the political process on their own behalf (one thinks of the contrast between traditional oligarchies in Latin America and social-democratic polities, such as Myrdal's own Sweden). Modern welfare state systems, in Myrdal's view, are more likely to pursue development policies that promote spread effects to less-developed regions of the country. In their abundance, developed economies induce the advantaged to accept policies of "rational generosity" and "bearable sacrifice" toward the less advantaged (1957:40–41). Political democracy and economic equity reinforce each other in a cycle of virtue, or so Myrdal hoped.

Have the public policies of modern democracies, such as the United States, succeeded in producing more equitable distributions of wealth and income over time? On a wider scale, has the world as a whole become more egalitarian in its distribution of resources? These are complicated and difficult questions, which we address in the appendix, and their answers depend largely on how we choose to define and measure inequality. In general, however, we may say that while both the United States and the world as a whole have become considerably more prosperous in recent decades, and some developing economies, such as those in China and India, have flourished, inequalities between the richest and poorest nations have generally grown wider. Meanwhile, economic inequalities within most nations—including the United States, China, and India—have also tended to widen (Firebaugh 2003:2152–66).[5]

FOUR

MATTHEW EFFECTS IN POLITICS AND PUBLIC POLICY

IN THIS CHAPTER we turn our attention from the economic to the political realm, focusing on how power tends to beget more power. Here, as in the previous chapter on cumulative economic advantage, we provide a wide array of illustrative examples of self-amplifying or deamplifying processes to convey a sense of the widespread and significant role that these play in political life. Each of the brief examples offers potential directions for further investigation of political Matthew effects.

Of course, we can never really separate economics from politics; the two are so closely intertwined that we often observe economic advantage being converted into political advantage, and vice versa.[1] Possessing wealth may permit political actors to invest money in accumulating political power and influence through strategic campaign contributions, expensive media campaigns, and the like. In turn, political power may enable actors to promote or prevent legislation affecting their financial interests. In this way, economic advantage can lead to further political advantage, and political advantage to further economic advantage, in an endless loop.

MATTHEW EFFECTS IN POLITICS

Self-amplifying cycles are commonplace in political life. Although political scientists rarely invoke the term *Matthew effect* to describe such cycles, much of their research is deeply relevant to the subject, and the field is fertile for further analysis of causally circular processes. Let us briefly consider some of the ways in which Matthew effects operate in the political sphere.

ACCUMULATING STATE POWER

Political history is fraught with instances of the use of state power to accumulate further state power. Wallerstein (1976/1980:232) offers this example:

> A state machinery involves a tipping mechanism. There is a point where strength creates more strength. The tax revenue enables the state to have a larger and more efficient civil bureaucracy and army which in turn leads to greater tax revenue—a process that continues in spiral form. The tipping mechanism works in the other direction too—weakness leads to greater weakness.

In effect, here the state operates like a profit-seeking corporation, investing some of its profits in maintaining and expanding mechanisms to extract further profit. The basic logic of capital accumulation is the same in either case, except that the state has readier access to the use of force in its pursuit of capital. The use of force often has been an effective tool to accumulate political resources, as the history of tyrannies has long taught.

ADVANTAGES OF INCUMBENCY

One of the clearest examples of Matthew effects in the sphere of democratic politics is seen in the advantages of incumbency. Political actors generally seek to use the advantages of their offices to secure more advantages. They invest power in the pursuit of more power, just as financial actors invest money in the pursuit of more money. Those who hold office have opportunities to build name recognition and cultivate fundraising connections that are not usually available to their challengers. Incumbents in the U.S. Senate can attract more than five times as much in campaign donations as their challengers, while incumbents in the U.S. House of Representatives can raise more than four times as much. It is not surprising that, since 1964, 81 percent of incumbents in the Senate and 93 percent in the House of Representatives have been reelected to office (Center for Responsive Politics 2005). Thus do the politically secure become more secure.

Why do incumbents have such a dramatic fundraising advantage? As office holders, they receive contributions based largely on their actual or perceived power to tip legislation in favor of one or another self-interested constituency. Interested donors invest in politicians somewhat as though they were stocks, and while a generous campaign contribution does not necessarily guarantee political access or influence (any more than a large investment in the stock market guarantees a profit), it increases the likelihood of access and influence. Challengers, for their part, may also attempt to raise funds on the implied promise of providing favors if elected, but this strategy works only when challengers appear to have a reasonable prospect of winning. The self-perpetuating advantages of incumbency tend to undermine such prospects.

BANDWAGON AND UNDERDOG EFFECTS

Another clear example of the operation of Matthew effects in electoral politics is the bandwagon effect, a term coined by Herbert Simon (1954) to describe the possible impact of polling results on election outcomes. Simon hypothesized that when polls show a candidate gaining momentum in an election campaign, some voters choose to hop onto that candidate's bandwagon in the hope of being on the winning side, thus accelerating the momentum of the candidate's campaign. Published polls and early election results may also discourage supporters of trailing candidates from voting at all. Simon considered the opposite possibility of an "underdog effect" as well, wherein some voters, feeling sympathy for a trailing candidate, may shift their support to that candidate. Subsequent research on the existence and strength of such polling effects has been mixed (Walden 1996:415–17), but generally shows that modest bandwagon effects sometimes occur, and tend to override underdog effects (Mehrabian 1998).

Even when such polling effects are small, they may tip the balance in close elections. They may also affect the ability of candidates to raise campaign contributions, as the horse that is expected to win the race generally attracts more bettors. In political fundraising, the saying goes that money follows money, meaning that the momentum or inertia of a fundraising campaign can create upward or downward spirals of donation. The more you raise, the more you raise; and conversely, the less you raise, the less you raise (Hulse and Herszenhorn 2008).

POLITICAL CORRUPTION

Legitimate campaign financing shades into corruption when political office holders or office seekers peddle influence for the sake of their own personal or political enrichment. Outright political bribery, vote buying, and other such practices enrich not only the politician, but also those who expect to profit from purchasing influence. Thus, bribery and other corrupt practices tend to amplify the advantages of the powerful and, simultaneously, the disadvantages of those who are too poor or powerless to afford the price. However, illicit practices of this sort are only effective so long as they remain clandestine. Once exposed, political corruption may backfire in the faces of its perpetrators, resulting in a sudden loss of power. Some Matthew effects, it seems, can operate only in the dark.

GERRYMANDERING

Political Matthew effects may also result from gerrymandering, or the partisan redrawing of electoral districts to advance the interests of a political party. This typically occurs when a party wins a legislative majority and proceeds to use its political authority to redraw the electoral map so as to improve its likelihood of achieving victory by an even larger margin in the next election. Both major political parties in the United States have played the gerrymandering game for many years—sometimes brazenly, as in the 2003 redistricting of Texas congressional districts by a Republican majority in the Texas state legislature under the guidance of U.S. House majority leader Tom DeLay (Toobin 2003). Through redistricting, Republicans sought to widen their margin of dominance even further in subsequent congressional elections.

CLASS ADVANTAGES IN THE JUSTICE SYSTEM

We find Matthew effects operating in both the civil and criminal divisions of the U.S. justice system. In both civil and criminal cases, individuals and organizations with vast resources can afford to hire expensive legal counsel far beyond the means of ordinary citizens. In *The Rich Get Richer and the Poor Get Prison,* Reiman (2001) describes a criminal justice system in which white-collar crimes are prosecuted less frequently and more leniently than less costly nonviolent street crimes. The result is an expanding prison system teeming with prisoners drawn overwhelmingly from the lowest economic classes. Reiman finds evidence of systemic class bias throughout the system:

> *For the same criminal behavior* [Reiman's emphasis], the poor are more likely to be arrested; if arrested they are more likely to be charged; if charged, more likely to be convicted; if convicted, more likely to be sentenced to prison; and if sentenced, more likely to be given longer prison terms than members of the middle and upper classes. (2001:110)

Class bias in the criminal justice system is interwoven with racial and ethnic bias in many jurisdictions, as in the common practice of racial profiling.

Prison is the gateway to a downward spiral for many young poor. Returning from prison to the streets hardened and demoralized, with a lack of employable skills compounded by the stigma of being ex-convicts (Goffman 1963), many leave the system more disadvantaged than when they entered, and with fewer of the resources needed for the long climb upward (Pager 2007). Many of them will return to prison, perpetuating the downward cycle. Even those stigmatized by relatively minor offenses, such as prostitution, may find that attempting to break free of the downward spiral is a painful and precarious process (Mansson and Hedin 1999). The grim underside of the Matthew effect is that disadvantage begets further disadvantage and, too often, criminality further criminality.

Law enforcement practices, even when well intentioned, may reinforce class inequalities. When criminologist Wesley Skogan (1990:107–09; in Sherman 1998) evaluated a community policing program in Houston, he found that whites and homeowners were more aware of the program than other groups, more likely to belong to the community organizations involved in it, and hence more apt to take advantage of it. Thus, while the program appeared to reduce overall victimization in the community, its benefits tended to flow to the neighborhood's most advantaged members. Skogan concluded that the program had inadvertently created a substantial Matthew effect, benefiting primarily white middle-class homeowners rather than the minority populations living in rental housing, for whose benefit the program was originally intended.

RACIAL AND ETHNIC INEQUALITIES

Matthew effects are also common in the arena of racial and ethnic relations. While we focus on the disadvantaged status of African Americans in the United States, similar dynamics affect the status of Hispanics and other disadvantaged ethnic groups as well.

Gunnar Myrdal (1944), in his classic analysis of American race relations, argued that minority group disadvantages reinforce white racial attitudes, and that these attitudes in turn reinforce minority disadvantages. Merton (1948) makes a similar argument in his famous essay on the self-fulfilling prophesy. Minority disadvantages in education, employment, and the like feed white stereotypes of minority inferiority, justifying discriminatory practices that deepen these very deficits (Knapp 1999). A vicious cycle is thus set into motion, in which racist beliefs among dominant groups perpetuate minority deprivation by diminishing minority opportunities, and minority deprivation is then interpreted as further confirmation of racist beliefs. In the absence of intervention to break this vicious cycle, the disadvantaged become more disadvantaged.

A vicious cycle also is evident in patterns of residential segregation associated with the phenomenon of white flight—or, more accurately, middle-class flight—from the problems of inner cities and their predominantly minority populations (see Palen 2005:120, 136–38, 193). As a result of flight, suburbs have prospered and their real estate has appreciated in value in relative terms, while increasingly segregated inner-city neighborhoods have grown relatively poorer. As home equity is the principal means of accumulating wealth for most families, black homeowners suffer disproportionately from this trend. Oliver and Shapiro (2006:9) observe that "the mean value of the average white home appreciates at a dramatically higher rate than the average black home." Matthew effects operating through residential segregation thus work to widen the economic and political divide between whites and blacks in American society.

Blacks face still other disadvantages in the real estate marketplace. Because they are disproportionately represented among lower-income potential homebuyers, they are more likely than others to be targeted for subprime mortgage loans, for which financial institutions may "charge borrowers higher interest rates, often requiring higher processing and closing fees, and often containing special load conditions like prepayment penalties, balloon payments, and adjustable interest rates" (Oliver and Shapiro 2006:217). These financial devices, known as predatory lending practices, threaten at every turn to catch the vulnerable in whirlpools of deepening debt and disadvantage. In housing, as in other consumer markets, the poor tend to pay more, whether the product in question is gasoline, utility deposits, car purchases, interest rates, or insurance premiums (Oliver and Shapiro 2006:223).

Income disparities further widen the divide between whites and blacks. Oliver and Shapiro (2006:75) note that "wealth accrues with increasing income because higher-earning groups accumulate wealth-producing assets at a faster pace," and that savings rates likewise increase with income. This pattern of increased investment and savings disproportionately benefits white households, the larger disposable incomes of which help to accelerate the advantages conferred by higher income alone.

Oliver and Shapiro rightly contend that wealth is a far more meaningful indicator of economic advantage than income (2006; see also Caner and Wolff 2004; Shapiro 2001; 2004). Two families may have identical incomes, but dramatically different wealth assets. Focusing on income to measure a family's economic status distorts our understanding of the profound differences in life chances and access to opportunity structures that exist between those who are wealthy and those of similar income who are not.

The wealth gap between blacks and whites in the United States is vastly wider than the income gap. As noted previously, the accumulated assets of black and Hispanic households are, on average, less than one-tenth that of white households (Kochlar 2004). Oliver and Shapiro (2006:4–6) offer several reasons for this pattern of extreme inequality. First, state policies from slavery onward have been racialized, tending to favor whites over blacks in the accumulation of wealth. Government policies after World War II promoted suburbanization through the funding of Federal Housing Administration (FHA) loans, which, early on, enforced restrictive covenants that prevented blacks from moving into new and overwhelmingly white suburban neighborhoods. The resulting racial segregation gave whites an advantage over blacks in building home equity. Other governmental policies, such as federal policies lowering capital gains taxes and allowing deductions for mortgage interest and property taxes (2006:44–47), have similarly benefited those who own substantial property at the expense of those who do not. Second, black businesses historically have been shut off from access to white markets, discouraging black entrepreneurship and self-employment, while white businesses have had relatively unhampered access to black markets. Finally, these and other factors, such as low wages and poor schooling, have converged to hinder blacks from accumulating financial advantages as readily as whites, thereby preventing them from passing on substantial assets from one generation to the next. Here the Matthew effect comes clearly into play. Inheriting assets tends to facilitate the accumulation of further assets with each succeeding generation, while the absence of inheritance tends to beget intergenerational poverty. Thus, many black families, coping with the challenge of daily survival, have been unable to save, let alone invest in accumulating significant wealth. Meanwhile, many white families have accumulated substantial assets and passed them on to their offspring, perpetuating a cycle of privilege while the less privileged have suffered the "accumulation of disadvantage . . . passed from generation to generation" (Wilson 1987:8).

Global labor markets and the resulting export of manufacturing jobs are another factor negatively affecting the African American community. When blue-collar jobs disappear from American cities, the resulting unemployment disproportionately affects minority communities (Wilson 1996), helping to account for the fact that black unemployment rates are typically more than twice that of whites. Unemployment often sets into motion a downward spiral of secondary effects, such as family instability and socially or personally destructive behavior, which only deepen the disadvantages of those who were already disadvantaged to begin with. Marital instability and a preponderance of single-parent households further reduce the possibility of saving and accumulating assets (Oliver and Shapiro 2006:76–78).

All these factors contribute to the widening gap between black and white asset formation. For some, these inequities call for concerted political action to combat the pernicious effects of cumulative racial advantage. Feagin (2006:4) has called for scholars to focus greater attention on the "intergenerational transmission of unjust enrichment and unjust impoverishment over centuries," resulting in the ongoing reproduction of white wealth, power, and privilege through the course of American history. He argues that the American economy has depended from its inception on extracting wealth from the labor of African Americans, and that this extracted wealth has been transmitted systemically from one generation of privileged whites to the next through deeply entrenched racist institutions bolstered by equally entrenched ideologies—ideologies which, as "sincere fictions" (2006:45), are conveniently invisible to those who hold them. He concludes that white advantage cannot be understood apart from black disadvantage; on the contrary, the latter has made the former possible.

In recent years, there has been movement among a determined band of policy analysts to redress the extreme racial and ethnic inequalities in wealth that persist in the United States. Federal policies have tended to favor the accumulation of assets by predominantly white middle- and upper-class Americans through incentives and subsidies for home ownership, college education, business development, and retirement savings (Boshara 2003; Woo, Schweke, and Buchholz 2004). Organizations such as the Ford Foundation and the Corporation for Enterprise Development, however, have proposed a number of policies to enhance the wealth-producing assets of African Americans and other disadvantaged groups, including poor whites, through the active involvement of both the public and private sectors (Shapiro 2004:184–202). Recommendations designed to assist the poor in asset building include, among other initiatives, the creation of children's savings accounts. In this proposal, each child in the United States would receive at birth an initial deposit ($1,000 in Shapiro's proposal, $6,000 in Boshara's) from government or private sources. In Shapiro's proposal, family deposits to the account would be matched over time and external contributions could be tied to such behaviors as academic achievement and graduation, community service, summer employment, and the development of financial literacy. Other proposed programs include forming similar accounts for disadvantaged adults (individual development accounts, or IDAs) and for purchasing homes (down payment accounts), since home ownership is the single most important means of asset building for most families. Policy analysts also have recommended reforming tax policies that have concentrated wealth increasingly in the hands of the few. Doing so would reverse the trend toward tax policies that systematically redistribute wealth upward, replacing these with tax policies that favor middle- and lower-income families and counteracting what Shapiro (2004:200) has called "our national drift toward plutocracy." Such policies would benefit members of racial and ethnic minorities, such as blacks and Hispanics, who are currently overrepresented among those who are asset poor, without discriminating against poor whites. It remains an open question whether these initiatives, if implemented, would adequately counteract the powerful historical force of Matthew effects, which have long tended to privilege the privileged.

ORGANIZATIONAL POLITICS

Matthew effects appear not only in the macro-level politics of group relations at the societal level (such as in the relations among classes or ethnic groups), but in the micro-level politics of organizations as well. Here we shift our attention from the distribution of wealth to the distribution of power. Power and authority relations exist in organizations of all kinds, and the use of power to expand power is not confined to the governmental sphere. It is found in the internal politics of diverse organizations, including corporations, schools, and religious bodies. Kanter (1977) observes that powerful members of organizations, by virtue of their positions, alliances, and relative freedom of operation, can accomplish more than those below them and, through these accomplishments, can expand their power bases. The lower echelons, on the other hand, find themselves trapped in "downward spirals of power" (1977:viii), desperately attempting to assert what little control they possess through petty territoriality, narrow rule-mindedness, and other ineffective strategies. "Power rises and falls," Kanter states (1977: 196–97), but at the individual level, "power is likely to bring more power, in ascending cycles, and powerlessness to generate powerlessness in a descending cycle."

Women, historically trapped at the lower levels of organizational life and taught to defer to powerful men, have only begun to reverse gendered Matthew effects, or what Rossiter (1993) calls Matilda effects, that have hindered their advancement in the past. Valian's (1999) extensive analysis of accumulated advantage and disadvantage in the professions, as previously noted, emphasizes that small initial differences in the performance evaluations of men and women are often amplified to produce large differences over time. To illustrate, she cites Martell, Lane, and Emrich's (1966) computer simulation of an eight-level corporate hierarchy in which slight male advantages at each level produce ever larger advantages in promotion at each higher level: In the model, an organization with equal numbers of males and females at the bottom level eventually becomes overwhelmingly male at the top. Valian (1999:303ff) proposes a variety of strategies that women can use to neutralize or reverse the Matthew effects of the past and gain greater power in organizations, including training decision makers to understand the concept of—and recognize instances of—cumulative advantage.

Will women in future positions of power use that power to promote more egalitarian organizations? There is some evidence that women are more likely than men to disapprove of extreme inequalities. When Tang (1996) asked men and women in his samples to allocate salaries in a hypothetical three-tiered organizational hierarchy, in which the salary of the second tier was set at $20,000, women proposed smaller salary differentials from top to bottom than did men. Tang interpreted these findings to mean that women are generally less approving of Matthew effects than men are.

In another study of Matthew effects in organizational life, Gabris and Mitchell (1988) found that merit-pay plans based on performance evaluations may unintentionally create Matthew effects in the morale of employees, improving the morale of those who receive high evaluations while angering, alienating, and causing even lower productivity among those whose performance is deemed most in need of improvement. Thus, Matthew effects may have ironic consequences in the workplace, undermining the intended effects of organizational policy.

LIFE CHANCES AND THE POLITICS OF HEALTH CARE

Matthew effects are also at work in the politics of health care. Here, as in virtually every other sphere of life, economic inequalities are crucial. They significantly shape one's life chances (Weber 1946 [1922]) and the varying degrees of access that people have to the opportunity structures that yield the good things in life—not only material goods, but also health and other dimensions of human well-being. Matthew effects can significantly affect the life chances of entire cohorts within a population. Dannefer (1987) has found that age cohorts tend to be-

come increasingly heterogeneous as they grow older, not only financially (as the rich grow richer at a faster rate than the less advantaged),
but in other respects including health conditions. This creates a Matthew effect, as the cumulative advantages of those who are better off
earlier in life pay high dividends later in life, including the dividend
of longer life expectancy for those with prior advantages. While older Americans as a group have never been more prosperous, this general prosperity masks widening economic disparities within the fifty-
and-over population since 1980 (Gist, Figueiredo, and Ng-Baumhackl
2001). Thus, Dannefer, alluding to Adam Smith's famous conviction
that a rising economic tide lifts all boats, notes that "there are trou-
bling signs that not all boats have been lifted by the rising tide of prosperity—and not all boats will stay afloat." Moreover, not everyone has
a boat, and some may drown even in the most prosperous of times
within social systems that permit extreme inequalities. Those without health insurance in particular, constituting more than 40 million
people in the United States, risk drowning for relative lack of access to
lifesaving medical resources.

Public policy can mitigate somewhat the effects of economic class
on life chances. A Canadian study (Dzakpasu, Joseph, Kramer, and
Allen 2000) reports that disparities in infant mortality rates among
socioeconomic groups since the 1960s have narrowed, due in part to
national health policies and programs. However, this "narrowing gap
in Canada contrasts with the international picture, where the opposite
has occurred, resulting in increasing disparities in infant mortality
between industrialized countries and other countries" (for a contrary
view, see Bishai and Poon 2001). In this wider international context,
the report notes, we find a "Matthew effect . . . wherein the magnitude
of improvement in the health status of a population over time appears
to be linked to the prior health of that population" and to its level of
economic development (Dzakpasu et al. 2000:e5).

Matthew effects have also been observed in the day-to-day practices of health-care delivery systems. In an analysis of the inpatient
population of New York state hospitals, Link and Milcarek (1980)
found that the distribution of mental health resources tended to favor patients who were most desirable (in the eyes of health provid-

ers) over those who were most in need. Institutions channeled care disproportionately toward younger, more motivated, more communicative, and more competent clients—in short, toward those who entered the system with personal and social advantages. At the other end of the spectrum, criminologist Wesley Skogan (1990:185–86) reports that "homeless street people with complicated mental, drug and alcohol problems" were typically not directed toward health care and rehabilitation, but rather "were dealt with in the only fashion the case system allowed—they were arrested." Each of these examples reflects a systemic bias in health care that helps the affluent to remain healthy as the poor grow sicker.

MATTHEW EFFECTS IN PUBLIC POLICY: THE CASE OF TAX LAW

Because Matthew effects are so pervasive in the political economy, democratic societies must find ways to rein in their worst excesses. Merton recognized this political imperative when he noted that vast inequalities between the most and least privileged segments of society produce "differential advantages for certain segments of the population, differentials that are not bound up with demonstrated differences in capacity" (1973 [1942]: 273). Extreme inequalities of condition produce corresponding inequalities of opportunity, as in each new generation, some inherit unearned advantages while others inherit unearned disadvantages (e.g., in nutrition, schooling, or access to influential networks). These inequalities of access to opportunity structures call forth "increasing regulation by political authority . . . to preserve and extend equality of opportunity [and] to put democratic values into practice" (Merton 1973 [1942]: 273).

Numerous public policies in the United States and Europe during the past century have been designed partly to redress extreme inequalities and thus mitigate Matthew effects. Policies in such areas as health care, education, and Social Security have been instituted to assist the least advantaged, though in practice the main beneficiaries of such policies often have been the middle classes (Deleeck, Van den Bosch, and Lathouwer 1992). Tax and labor policies during the Progressive Era, for example, included progressive income and estate taxation, representing a step toward addressing the stark inequities of the Gilded Age. The New Deal ushered in Social Security, the Works Progress Administration (WPA) and the Civilian Conservation Corps (CCC), among other programs, in an effort to prevent the poor from becoming poorer during the Great Depression. Following World War II, federal initiatives such as the G.I. Bill and FHA/Veteran Affairs (VA) housing loans created opportunities for advancement among veterans who might otherwise have been left behind. In the 1960s, Great Society programs, such as Medicare, Medicaid, affirmative action, and Aid to Families with Dependent Children (AFDC) further attempted to provide safety nets and economic opportunities for large segments of the population, including the elderly, the poor, and historically subjugated minorities. It is beyond our scope to examine these policies in detail, but for illustrative purposes, it is useful to focus briefly on one body of public policy in particular—tax policy—and its relevance to an understanding of Matthew effects.

PROGRESSIVE AND REGRESSIVE TAXATION

Debates over tax policy raise numerous philosophical questions. Legal philosophers Murphy and Nagel (2002) have explored many of these questions in some detail. What is a fair tax? What is economic justice and what is taxation's role in achieving it? Should taxes be redistributive? In what proportions should their burdens fall upon more and less advantaged segments of the population? How should the issue of inheritance be dealt with? How are issues of taxation bound up with larger issues of politics and the common good? How we answer such questions says a good deal about who we are, both personally and as a society.

Near the heart of the questions is the issue of redistribution. All taxation is, in a sense, a redistribution of resources from some segments of society to others. A progressive tax levies higher average rates on those with more wealth or income. Progressive taxes hit hardest those who can most afford to pay them, generally redistributing a society's resources downward from more to less privileged segments of the population.

A regressive tax is redistributive in the opposite direction: It levies higher average rates on those with less wealth or income. Regressive taxes hit hardest those who can least afford to pay them, generally redistributing resources upward. The federal income tax, at least in principle, is progressive, though in practice a skilled tax lawyer or accountant can often find ways short of illegal evasion to avoid paying some, or in rare instances all, of the taxes scheduled to be paid by those in high income brackets (Bartlett and Steele 2000; Johnston 2003). A sales tax is regressive: While rich and poor pay exactly the same flat rate on the purchase of the same consumer good, the poor must spend a much larger proportion of their wealth and income on consumption merely to survive, while the rich can save and invest a larger proportion of theirs. Thus the sales tax takes a larger proportion of the resources of the poor. Consider, too, that the same dollar means more to a poor person than to a rich one. To a poor person, the dollar may be the difference between eating and going hungry, while to the rich person, a single dollar is of almost no consequence.

It is often noted that, because federal income taxes in the United States are progressive in principle, upper income groups shoulder a disproportionate share of the tax burden. It is true that the upper classes as a whole contribute a substantial proportion of federal income taxes. In 2000, the richest 1 percent of taxpayers, those with adjusted gross incomes exceeding $313,000, earned nearly 21 percent of all reported income but paid more than 37 percent of individual federal income taxes (Johnston 2003:11). If federal income taxes were the only taxes anyone paid, our tax system would be fairly described as progressive. However, when we consider not just all federal taxes, including the regressive Social Security tax, but state and local taxes as well, including regressive sales and excise taxes as well as property taxes, which tend to be higher in per dollar valuation in poor neighborhoods than in rich ones, we find that the overall tax burden in the United States is almost flatly distributed among income groups. The Bureau of Labor Statistics reports that in 2001, the most advantaged one-fifth of Americans paid 19 percent of their incomes in taxes of all kinds, while the poorest one-fifth paid 18 percent (Johnston 2003:94).

Other sources of state revenue, such as lottery revenue, are also steeply regressive, preying upon those who are not savvy enough to know that, as the joke goes, the lottery is a tax on people who are bad at math. A recent study by the Texas Lottery Commission found that while those with higher incomes and more education are more likely to participate in the lottery, those with lower incomes and less education gamble away far more money (Casey 2005). In effect, the lottery resembles a voluntary but steeply regressive tax that benefits the state while impoverishing its poorest and least-educated citizens.

Despite the relative progressivity of the federal income tax, many features of our tax system favor middle- and upper-income citizens. The homeowner subsidy benefits primarily middle- and upper-income Americans, and tax expenditures on higher education amount to public subsidies of colleges and universities attended primarily by the offspring of middle- and upper-class families. Bartlett and Steele (2000) and Johnston (2003) argue that enforcing tax laws also tends to favor upper income groups. With the aid of tax attorneys and accountants, upper class taxpayers can effectively hide or shelter assets, fabricate questionable deductions, and create complicated financial arrangements, legally or not, in the gray and virtually impenetrable miasma created by the sheer complexity of our tax codes. These practices make it exceedingly difficult for the Internal Revenue Service (IRS) to detect and prosecute tax fraud. Funds to enforce tax laws have been cut back in recent years, resulting in a "rampant and growing" tax-cheating problem in the upper income brackets (Johnston 2003:294). Scarce tax enforcement resources are focused increasingly on investigating the working poor, especially those who claim the earned income tax credit (2003:129ff).

The upshot, Johnston concludes, is that the federal tax system, envisioned by Theodore Roosevelt as a guard against a financial aristocracy of "malefactors of great wealth," in practice often protects and even increases concentrations of wealth, creating several Matthew effects:

> Chief executives use tax-deductible dollars from their corporate trea-
> suries to pay [tax specialists] to develop and refine techniques that
> enable executives to delay paying their taxes—not from December to
> January, but for years, even decades. Invest those deferred taxes year
> after year and soon an economic snowball starts rolling, with one's
> wealth growing faster and faster (thanks to the magic of compound in-
> terest) until a great fortune is built, like the billion dollars of untaxed
> wealth amassed by the Coca-Cola executive, Robert Goizueta. Defer-
> ral, the tax lawyers say, is 90 percent of tax planning. Delay a tax for 30
> years and its cost in today's money is almost nothing. Inflation and un-
> paid tax should cover the bill. (Johnston 2003:117)

At the other end of the spectrum, Johnston examines the prosecution
of the working poor for suspected abuse of the earned income tax
credit. He notes that in 2002, more than half the 744,000 individual
tax returns that the IRS audited were filed by the working poor, who
represent less than 17 percent of taxpayers (2003:134). He recounts the
case of Ms. Reyes, a cleaning woman in Los Angeles whom the IRS
accused of fraud and required to return several years of credits. Ms.
Reyes went "into a panic because she knew that she could never pay
it back, that the interest would grow and grow, ruining any hope she
might have to ever get ahead despite her lack of education" (2003:133).
Thus the mathematics of compound interest creates an upward spiral
of wealth for the corporate executive, but a downward spiral of debt
for the cleaning woman.

INCOME TAX REFORM

Critics of the existing federal income tax system have advanced a
range of proposals for tax reform. Conservatives have generally favored reforms that would result in a less progressive tax structure.
Federal income tax cuts enacted during the George W. Bush administration were widely criticized for primarily benefiting upper income
groups, shifting the overall tax burden downward to the middle classes. Liberals, by contrast, tend to favor progressive reforms that would
shift the tax burden upward, a strategy that conservatives disparag-
ingly call "soaking the rich."

Among the most controversial tax reform proposals is the flat tax, proposed by Hall and Rabushka (1995) and embraced by former Republican presidential hopefuls Steve Forbes and Jack Kemp, among others. Hall and Rabushka envision a simplified national tax to replace the massively complex federal income tax code. They propose an across-the-board income tax on wages, exempting returns on savings, such as interest, dividends, and capital gains, as well as gifts and inheritances. Their plan, like most plans of this type, would impose a flat rate (e.g., 20 percent) on all income that exceeds a specified amount (e.g., $20,000) to avoid imposing undue hardship on the poor. As the first $20,000 of income is tax-free, the flat tax is not truly flat. In a narrow sense, it is a progressive tax, as it taxes those who make more than $20,000 at a higher rate than those who make less. A closer look, however, reveals that most flat tax proposals are actually regressive. By taxing wage income but not income from investment, inheritance, and other sources enjoyed primarily by the upper classes, the flat tax is essentially a tax on work. According to one estimate, working-class taxpayers would pay more under a flat tax system than under a moderately progressive tax, such as the current federal income tax (McCaffery 2002:51). Meanwhile, wealthy citizens would pay substantially less than they do under the current system (Kinsley 1995).

McCaffery (2002) has proposed a fair tax as an alternative to the flat tax proposal. The fundamental difference between a flat tax and a fair tax is that, while the former is essentially a simplified income tax, the latter is a sales tax on consumption, usually proposed as an alternative to the income tax. McCaffery's fair tax, like the flat tax, would tax earned income but exclude returns on savings (investment, dividends, and capital gains), gifts, and inheritance. Thus, it would be, in effect, a consumption tax on all income spent and not saved. Unlike the flat tax, however, the fair tax would institute, through a national sales or value-added tax, a progressive rate structure that would tax those who spend more at higher rates than those who spend less. For example, the first $20,000 of spending might be exempt from taxes, with the next $60,000 taxed at 10 percent, the following $80,000 at 20 percent, and so on. Spending of more than $1,000,000 per year would be taxed at a maximum rate of 50 percent (2002:26). This proposal, like the flat tax proposal, would drastically simplify the tax code and would encourage savings, yet McCaffery contends that it would place a heavier burden on the rich than on the poor, which most Americans agree is morally appropriate. McCaffery further argues that such a simplified tax, while not dramatically altering the distribution of the existing tax burden, could increase rates of compliance and thus reduce the social costs of tax evasion. McCaffery presents his plan as a compromise between conservative proposals, such as the regressive flat tax, and liberal calls for greater progressivity in the tax system.

Not everyone is sold, however, on the fairness of fair tax plans (e.g., Graetz and Shapiro 2005:273–77). Some remain skeptical of the fairness and progressivity of a plan that shields accumulated wealth (e.g., investments, inheritance) from all taxation, thereby protecting and fortifying great fortunes while taxing the essential daily consumption expenditures of middle- and working-class citizens. We noted previously that, in general, the greater one's wealth or income, the smaller is the proportion of that income devoted to consumption. The poor must spend nearly all their income on basic survival needs, such as food and housing, while the rich can afford to devote a larger share of their resources to investments that stand to enrich them even further. This creates a Matthew effect that both flat and fair tax plans would only intensify by dramatically reducing or eliminating taxes on invested wealth.

ESTATE TAX REFORM

Flat and fair tax proposals are among the arsenal of political strategies employed by those who seek to eliminate all taxes on estates and inheritances. Since the Progressive Era, there has been a broad public consensus that progressive taxation, including taxes on the inheritance of great fortunes, is morally fair and just. Extreme concentrations of wealth and power had marked the Gilded Age (1880–1900), when the legendary robber barons accumulated vast private fortunes and used these as leverage to promote their financial interests in the halls of government. Theodore Roosevelt and other Progressives soon rose to challenge excessive accumulations of wealth as a threat to the ideals of democracy. But the idea of progressive taxation did not begin with Roosevelt. Thomas Jefferson, Benjamin Franklin, Thomas Paine, and others had voiced similar ideas early on in American history, and the French aristocrat Alexis de Tocqueville, visiting the new republic in the 1830s, had observed in *Democracy in America* that the "American experiment presupposes a rejection of inherited privilege" (in Gates and Collins 2002:27–29). Roosevelt and the Progressives were only putting into practice, through the Sixteenth Amendment (1913) and the subsequent passage of progressive income, estate and gift taxes, principles that expressed a long-standing American mistrust of concentrations of wealth and power.

Since the rise of the conservative movement in the 1980s, progressive taxation has been under attack from the right. This attack has occurred, paradoxically, at a time when the gulf between rich and poor is widening steadily and relative concentrations of wealth are approaching Gilded Age levels. While the alternative minimum tax (Johnston 2003:95ff), instituted in 1969, is arguably progressive and increasingly affects upper-middle class taxpayers who fall under its provisions due to bracket creep, many other tax policies have become increasingly regressive. The tax rate on capital gains, which account for more than half the income of the very wealthy, fell from 28 percent in 1987 to 20 percent in 1998, and again to 15 percent in 2003 (2003:40). Conservative tax activists continue to work for total elimination of the capital gains tax.

Meanwhile, conservatives succeeded in passing a tax bill in 2001 that called for the gradual phaseout of the federal estate tax by 2010. The political history of this legislative campaign is told in fascinating detail by Graetz and Shapiro (2005), recounting right-wing strategists' ingenious tactics to win public support for the phaseout. The estate tax was cleverly relabeled the death tax, even though it is not a tax on the deceased. Its burden falls only on inheritors of very large fortunes, who receive the estate as new income. As one wag put it, "the estate tax is not a tax on Conrad Hilton. It's a tax on Paris Hilton."

Although the estate tax applied only to the richest 2 percent of estates, Americans widely believed that the tax applied to smaller estates and put many family farms and businesses in jeopardy. Liberal attempts to counter these public perceptions were too little and too late.

Following passage of the bill, however, a group of wealthy citizens, led by William Gates Sr., father of Bill Gates Jr., in collaboration with the Boston-based organization Responsible Wealth, launched a campaign to press vigorously for restoration of the estate tax (Gates and Collins 2002). Their appeal, echoing the sentiments of Thomas Jefferson, Andrew Carnegie, Theodore Roosevelt, and others, appealed to the essential fairness of preventing great concentrations of wealth and power in a democratic society. Gates and others fear that our nation is in danger of abandoning its historic commitment to equality of opportunity by allowing and even encouraging the formation of a hereditary financial aristocracy that will pass its economic advantages on to descendents who may have done nothing to earn them.

Policy proposals to abolish the estate tax, eliminate the capital gains tax, and reduce or eliminate the progressive federal income tax, while relying increasingly on regressive taxation to fund public purposes, all have the likely effect of accelerating rather than restraining economic Matthew effects. Efforts to reverse affirmative action laws and other social policies designed to create opportunities for the less advantaged are also likely, intentionally or not, to expand the opportunity structures of the already advantaged. It is urgent that we ask whether such policies and their probable consequences are consistent with our core values—if we can decide what these core values are, and whether greater equality is among them.

FIVE

MATTHEW EFFECTS IN EDUCATION AND CULTURE

ADVANTAGE TENDS TO beget further advantage, and disadvantage further disadvantage, not only in the economic and political spheres, but in the other spheres as well, including the realms of cognition and culture. Let us consider first the rather large body of literature that has accumulated on Matthew effects in the fields of education and developmental psychology.

MATTHEW EFFECTS IN EDUCATION

Merton (1988:614) noted Matthew effects in education, citing the well-known research of Robert Rosenthal and others (e.g., Burstall 1978; Rosenthal and Jacobson 1968) investigating the operation of self-fulfilling prophesies in the classroom. In his classic initial study, Rosenthal administered intelligence tests to a population of elementary school students at the beginning of the school year. He then selected 20 percent of these students at random and informed—or actually, misinformed—their classroom teachers that the students had been identified as "bloomers," who could be expected to make exceptional progress in the coming year. Rosenthal revisited the classes at the end of the year, retesting the students to measure improvement in student performance. He found that students who had been randomly labeled as bloomers showed significantly more progress than those who had not. Rosenthal interpreted this to mean that more is expected of students who are believed to be brighter, and that these higher expectations lead students to perform at higher than usual levels. Conversely, less is expected of those who are thought to be duller, and these lower expectations, in turn, produce lower levels of performance. Those labeled as bright get brighter, relative to a control group, even when there are no significant initial differences between the respective groups.

Subsequent studies have examined the possible role of Matthew effects in the cognitive development of children, particularly in their reading abilities (Bast and Reitsma 1997; 1998; Berninger 1999; Cunningham and Stanovich 1998; Shaywitz et al. 1995; Stanovich 1986; 1993; Walberg and Tsai 1983). In reading research, the Matthew effect refers to the hypothesis that "while good readers gain new skills very rapidly, and quickly move from 'learning to read' to 'reading to learn,' poor readers become increasingly frustrated with the act of reading, and try to avoid reading when possible. The gap is relatively narrow when the children are young, but rapidly widens as children grow older" (SEDL 2001). In short, "the word-rich get richer while the word-poor get poorer" in their reading skills (CASL 2001) and life chances generally.

Developmental psychologists agree that native abilities interact with environmental advantages or disadvantages in the development of reading skills. Students who begin with high verbal aptitudes and find themselves in verbally enriched social environments are at a double advantage. Moreover, early success tends to create a virtuous cycle, in which the young reader learns to read faster, more, and with better comprehension, building on early advantage to achieve even larger advantages relative to peers (Nuttall 1996:127). Meanwhile, students with more limited verbal aptitudes who also experience economic and social disadvantages are hit with a "double whammy" (Stanovich 1986:383), which may well affect their later life chances in the reading-intensive environment of an information society. Children who read slowly and without enjoyment read less (Stanovich 1986). Poor readers are more likely than good readers to drop out of school and less likely to find rewarding employment. Thus, reading disadvantages are often compounded, translating into economic and personal disadvantages; whether or not young students experience a reading spiral may affect not just their educational futures, but also their social and economic futures (Cunningham and Stanovich 1998). There may be a social dimension involved as well, as good readers may choose friends who also read avidly while poor readers seek friends with whom they share other enjoyments. It seems likely that the cognitive and social dynamics of reading education are also at work in mathematics education, as the numerate build on early advantages to become more numerate while those who have difficulty with numbers fall farther and farther behind (Bahr 2007).

Relatively few studies have tested the Matthew effect hypothesis over time to determine empirically whether the gap between good readers and poor readers in fact widens in fanlike fashion over time. Shaywitz and his colleagues (1995) find a small widening of differences in measured intelligence through time, but not in reading per se, while Bast and Reitsma (1998) find increasing differences for word recognition skills, but not for reading comprehension. Measured Matthew effects in reading seem to vary from strong (Awaida and Beech 1995; Howley 2001) to modest (Bast and Reitsma 1998) to minimal (Shaywitz et al. 1995) depending on the study's variables and methodologies. Researchers generally agree, however, that early differences between good readers and poor readers tend to persist into adulthood, and that poor readers rarely catch up. Howley (2001)[1] defends the position that the "effects appear to be profound: relatively small differences in reading ability and literacy-related knowledge and skills at the beginning of school often develop into very large generalized differences in school-related skills and academic achievement." In such "chaotic" processes, small differences in initial states can lead to great differences in final states. Matthew effects inhere in acquiring not only reading skills, but language-related knowledge and skills in general, including math skills (Bahr 2007). Thus, educational Matthew effects may be operating across many different dimensions of cognitive development.

Matthew effects also arise in the acquisition of computer skills. Moureau (1987) observes that the more computer experts are called upon to exercise their skills, the more they learn, and the more expert they become. Similarly, Sligo (1997) finds that organizational employees with more education become more aware of computer information resources and use them more effectively than those with less education do, widening their relative advantage over the latter.

Kerckhoff and Glennie (1999) examine Matthew effects in American education at the institutional level, gauging the effects of tracking, or the practice of channeling high-performing and low-performing students into separate curricula in public schools. Educational systems in Europe commonly assign high- and low-performing students to different schools; the American system reaches similar results by creating academic and vocational tracks within the same school. Kerckhoff and Glennie, following a cohort of tenth graders over ten years, report that tracking in high school tended to deflect lower-position students downward and upper-position students upward in their educational outcomes, dispersing the cohort more widely over time. They interpret these results as confirming the Matthew effect.

In his influential book *Savage Inequalities*, Kozol (1991) puts the pedagogical issues squarely into a larger societal context, arguing that the advantages and disadvantages of individual learners are largely a function of their economic environments. Kozol vividly describes the stark contrasts between impoverished inner city schools and their wealthier suburban counterparts. While he does not use the term *Matthew effect* explicitly to describe downward spirals of poverty and upward spirals of affluence in the American public school system, he offers numerous relevant examples of these phenomena.

Inner-city schools, Kozol observes, are caught up in a complex of mutually reinforcing problems associated with poverty, including high unemployment and crime rates in the surrounding community, industrial and middle-class flight, and family instability. Compounding these problems is the problem of underfunded schools. Public education in the United States is funded primarily through local property taxes, and low property valuations in poor neighborhoods necessitate higher tax rates, which residents can ill afford to pay. The result is that funding per pupil is dramatically lower in poor urban schools than in wealthier suburban schools. Kozol observes a Matthew effect at work here:

In effect, a circular phenomenon evolves: The richer districts—those in which the property lots and houses are more highly valued—have more revenue, derived from taxing land and homes, to fund their public schools. The reputation of the schools, in turn, adds to the value of their homes, and this, in turn, expands the tax base for public schools. (1991: 121)

While state governments generally supplement local tax revenues to make the funding of poor and rich school districts more equal, full equality is rarely if ever achieved. Suburban schools tend to spend more per pupil, enjoy better facilities, and attract better-qualified teachers and better-prepared students. Their students advance academically while students in poorer schools fall ever farther behind. And because learning is sequential, building on previous learning, those who fall behind at an early age may be permanently disadvantaged. The result, Kozol maintains, is the survival of the most favored, or in the words of John Coons, "the cyclical replacement of the 'fittest' of one generation by their artificially advantaged offspring" (1991:60, 206).

Efforts to redress inequalities in public schools meet resistance from those who benefit most from unequal funding. Critics disparage efforts toward equalization as Robin Hood measures (perhaps it is a sign of our times that Robin Hood, once portrayed as a hero, is now cast as a villain). They fear that more equitable funding of poorer schools at the expense of richer ones will erode educational quality; equality for all will mean excellence for none (1991:173). True improvements would require, among other things, massive increases in funding to urban school districts to bring them up to suburban levels, but this could only be accomplished by increasing taxes or defunding competing governmental priorities, neither of which is often a popular option.

Though Kozol does not address the issue specifically, a similar dynamic appears in the relation between public and private education. When educationally concerned and involved parents withdraw their children to private schools, often for understandable reasons, public school systems lose one of their most important resources. In general, private schools benefit and public schools suffer from this migration, creating a vicious cycle in which the further deterioration of public schools leads to further so-called bright flight to private schools. The potential result is a widening gulf between public and private education. Some have proposed to fund education publicly through voucher systems, permitting students to spend their vouchers in either public or private schools. Proponents argue that vouchers would create new opportunities for students trapped in poor public schools and force these schools to improve in order to retain students. Opponents worry, however, that such systems would allow private schools to cherry-pick the best students from public schools and leave poorer students behind, amplifying educational inequalities.

Social inequalities amplified by Matthew effects have been identified not only in primary and secondary education, but in higher education as well. Selingo and Brainard (2006) report in *The Chronicle of Higher Education* that by "almost every statistical measure, the divide between the haves and have-nots in education—among students as well as institutions—is growing. . . . Never before has a college degree meant more in determining social class in America." They note that wealthy colleges and universities not only raise more money than less advantaged institutions do each year, but also plow more back into their endowments, enabling them to enjoy larger returns on their investments. This elite stratum of institutions, drawing students overwhelmingly from upper-income households, continues to provide students with privileged access to elite social networks that further facilitate their advancement throughout life.

Numerous books in recent years have examined higher education's role in shaping the distribution of social advantage in the United States (Delbanco 2007). Perhaps the most prominent of these is *Equity and Excellence in American Higher Education* (Bowen, Kurzweil, and Tobin 2005). Former Princeton president William Bowen and his colleagues have amassed a wealth of historical and contemporary data bearing upon both the quality and social diversity of U.S. colleges and universities—diversity not only among the institutions themselves, but also among the populations they serve. The authors give high marks to American higher education for the quality of its instruction and research, especially among top institutions, but are far less satisfied with the equity of access that talented but economically disadvantaged students have to these institutions. The authors explicitly acknowledge how Matthew effects help to reproduce educational inequalities, citing the work of both Merton and Myrdal on cumulative advantage (2005:376). They observe that "it is the accumulation of (often small) advantages and disadvantages over the course of the first 18 years of life that leads to massive preparation differences by the time of college application," and that both disadvantages and advantages are "cumulative and reinforcing" (2005:225). The authors report that "the odds of getting into the pool of credible candidates for admission to a selective college or university are *six* times higher for a child from a high-income family than for a child from a poor family," and similarly, the odds are "*seven* times higher for a child from a college-educated family than for a child who would be a first-generation college-goer" (2005:248; authors' emphasis). To counteract the self-perpetuating cycle of advantage and disadvantage, Bowen and his colleagues recommend a form of "class-based affirmative action" (2005:178) that benefits the disadvantaged, in contrast to hidden forms of affirmative action that have historically benefited the sons and daughters of the advantaged, such as admissions policies favoring legacies, the children of wealthy donors, and families without financial need.

Matthew effects in higher education also operate among institutions. Academic institutions, like individuals, are stratified in American society, and there is no shortage of attempts to rank them against each other along a multitude of dimensions, including peer assessments, retention and graduation rates, student-faculty ratios, student class ranks and scores on standardized tests, acceptance rates, and alumni giving rates. Competition for institutional prestige is intense because prestige attracts further resources, such as donations, which may then be invested to further burnish an institution's reputation. And as Trow (1984:158; in Hearn 1991) observes, the "advantages of elite institutions are so overwhelming that they create what is for them (but perhaps not for the rest of higher education or the larger society) a kind of 'virtuous circle' in which advantage begets advantage."

Among the most successful institutions, this cycle of reputation and riches results in the accumulation of ever-larger institutional endowments. The size of a university's endowment is a powerful measure of its capacity to attract top scholars and students, and provide them with facilities and resources that enable the institution to attract still more resources, setting into motion a Matthew effect. It is not surprising that financial inequality among academic institutions in the United States is growing. Thornton (2007:23–26) writes that "we observe increasing differences between the endowments of rich and poor institutions, between the salaries of college and university presidents and their faculties, between the salaries of athletic coaches and professors, and between well and poorly compensated faculty members." She notes that the gap between more and less advantaged institutions has widened as richer institutions can afford to risk investment in higher-yield assets. The largest endowments realized a 15.7 percent average one-year rate of return in 2006–07—nearly double the return rate for the smallest endowments.

THE ACCUMULATION OF CULTURAL CAPITAL

Education in its broadest sense encompasses the fundamental knowledge, skills, beliefs, and values—in short, the culture—that we learn as members of social communities. The late French sociologist Pierre Bourdieu (1984; 1986) proposed that knowledge, skills, and even aesthetic tastes constitute a kind of cultural capital, analogous to economic capital, which social actors employ to maintain and improve their positions in society. Like economic capital, cultural capital can be inherited and reproduced from generation to generation, and can be accumulated through time.

Other Matthew effects known to operate in the economic sphere, such as the accelerating accumulation of principal through compound interest, have their counterparts in the cultural sphere as well. There is some evidence that Matthew effects operate in the religious sphere, where Broughton and Mills (1980) find that inequalities in the resources of Protestant clergy, as measured by the size, expenditures, and staff of their congregations, tend to grow wider as clergy age. Matthew effects are evident in the accumulation of cultural capital generally. Those who inherit large cultural advantages, such as access to elite schools and generous resources, are in a privileged position to turn these advantages to still further advantage. Those without such access are at a severe competitive disadvantage.

That said, the accumulation of cultural capital may have positive as well as negative functions; this was a principal finding of Merton and others in early research on Matthew effects in the sciences, as reported in Chapter 2. Merton argued that Matthew effects help to identify and publicize the achievements of top scientists, benefiting the scientific community as a whole by helping to maintain standards of excellence. Following Merton, Murray (2003:93–94, 353, 443) argues that Matthew effects may contribute not only to the cultural enrichment of the sciences, but to the enrichment of entire civilizations. In an ambitious attempt to identify factors that account for the emergence and recognition of great artists, scientists, and philosophers, Murray counts Matthew effects among the factors that help to identify and publicize the achievements of major cultural figures throughout history, preserving their achievements for future generations. Murray helps to remind us that while Matthew effects often have negative consequences, they may have broad positive consequences as well.

Closely akin to Bourdieu's notion of cultural capital is another form of noneconomic capital, which he terms symbolic capital—that is, social honor or prestige, which in our times often takes the form of celebrity. Like money and knowledge, prestige feeds upon itself. Consider the dynamics of fame. In our commercial culture, talent agents create synergies among mass media, parlaying a record contract into a television appearance and a television appearance into a magazine cover as they seek to propel their clients to greater heights of fame. Through the contagion of celebrity, the famous become more famous—at least for a time—until they are finally eclipsed by brighter lights.

The operation of Matthew effects in marketing celebrities and their products is brilliantly explored in an experiment (Salganik, Dodds, and Watts 2006; Watts 2007) in which the investigators registered more than 14,000 participants at a music website and invited them to listen to, rate, and, if they wished, download songs by unknown bands. Some participants could see only the names of the bands and their songs, while the remaining participants, broken into eight subgroups, or worlds, could also see which songs others in their world were downloading. Interestingly, "the particular songs that became hits were different in different worlds, just as cumulative-advantage theory would predict" (Watts 2007). In each world, early adopters seemed to influence the downloading choices of later adopters, creating Matthew effects that made some songs winners and others losers; yet the winners and losers in this market competition differed markedly from one world to the next. The headline of Watts' fascinating account of this experiment asks a tantalizing question: Is Justin Timberlake a product of cumulative advantage? The results of the experiment suggest that in other worlds, with different path-dependent histories of cumulative advantage, our own world's celebrities might now be languishing in obscurity.

Bourdieu identifies a third form of noneconomic capital, which he calls social capital,[2] deriving from the actor's location within networks of social power. Consider the role of elite university networks in promoting their members' interests. Access to elite institutions leads to other forms of social access, and to participation in economic and political networks that facilitate the further accumulation of social and cultural capital in Bourdieu's sense. It is noteworthy that in the six presidential elections from 1988 to 2008, every Republican and Democratic candidate for president except one was a graduate of either Harvard, Yale, or both. One such candidate was a mediocre student who relied on family political and economic connections to gain access first to Yale College and later to Harvard Business School before tapping family resources to enter the oil business (Kinsley 2001). He ascended eventually to the highest office in the land, largely through the power of Matthew effects.

The various forms of capital are intricately intertwined and mutually enriching. Although economic, cultural, symbolic, and social capital are analytically distinct from one another, they are not empirically independent of each other. Money can purchase a certain measure of power, prestige, and social connection, and likewise, non-economic forms of capital can often be invested in ways that pay economic dividends. The currency of one kind of capital is frequently convertible into the currency of another. Thus, when we study Matthew effects, we must think not only about how advantages in education beget further educational advantages, but also how they beget further economic, political, and cultural advantages.

SIX

IMPLICATIONS AND CONCLUSIONS

THIS BOOK HAS examined the literature on Matthew effects across a broad range of disciplines and institutional settings. It is time now to step back and ask some final, more philosophical questions. Are Matthew effects inevitable in social life, expressing laws of nature over which we have no control, or are they social constructions, which we ourselves have created and can alter or abolish? Are Matthew effects necessarily unjust or immoral in their consequences, or do they sometimes produce social benefits? When they are clearly harmful, do we have a moral responsibility to intervene? What countervailing forces, both natural and artificial, can limit or even override Matthew effects in human societies? Finally, what are some implications of Matthew effects for the future of inequality?

THE MATTHEW EFFECT: NATURAL LAW OR SOCIAL CONSTRUCT?

Are Matthew effects natural and unavoidable? Consider this parable from our own backyard. In our household live two miniature dachshunds. Brownie and Cinnamon are from the same litter, though Brownie, a male, is somewhat larger than his twin sister. Suppose that when I feed the dogs each morning, I put roughly the same amount of food in their dishes. Brownie eats quickly, and he has soon eaten his share of the food. At this point he nudges his slower-eating sister aside and eats as much food as he can from her bowl, growling her away if she tries to stop him. Without intervention, what is likely to happen? Larger and stronger to begin with, Brownie will grow even larger and stronger over time. He will use his initial advantage in size and strength to consume an increasingly disproportionate share of the food. Meanwhile, Cinnamon will slowly starve to death.

Sloman and Dunham (2004) have examined Matthew effects of this kind in biological competition within species; such effects, they argue, result from "difference amplification," which the authors define as "the process whereby baseline differences between two competing members of the same group are magnified by the outcome of competition" (2004:92). This process leads to an adaptive cycle of success for the winner and a maladaptive cycle of failure for the loser, reinforcing hierarchies of dominance and subordination within many species. Small genetic differences are amplified through intraspecific competition, conferring higher status on dominant males and giving them privileged access to valued resources. Dominant males also have privileged access to breeding females, which promotes the differential survival of their genes.

Sloman and Dunham speculate that the dynamics of difference amplification were at play among early human hunter-gatherers. Assortative mating, or the "tendency for people to choose mates that resemble each other in some key domain such as intelligence, physical appearance or height," (2004:99), typically results in patterns of mate selection whereby those with favored genes are likely to choose partners who also have favored genes. Through this process of sexual selection, the genetically rich tend to produce advantaged offspring. Dominant males thus secure advantages not only for themselves, but for their progeny as well. Assortative mating is also observed among the economically and socially advantaged in human societies, with high earners tending to marry other high earners while low earners tend to marry other low earners, exacerbating economic inequalities among households (Douthat and Salam 2005).

Matthew effects of this kind are but one variety of positive feedback loop found in nature.[1] Population explosions are another. These occur when fertility rates exceed mortality rates through time, setting into motion a pattern of accelerating population growth. Crespi (2004) examines several such loops as they have occurred during major evolutionary and ecological transitions. He notes that evolutionary biologists and ecologists generally have paid more attention to negative (stabilizing) than to positive (destabilizing) feedback loops. There is no doubt that negative feedback loops are important to maintaining equilibrium in natural systems, expressed in such phenomena as evolutionarily stable strategies, ecosystem stability, and homeostasis, but Crespi argues that positive feedback processes are also important in nature and are more common than biologists usually suppose. He contends that the "self-reinforcing dynamics" of positive feedback often generate the conditions for change in living systems.

From a naturalistic perspective, the feedback loops known as Matthew effects thus may be viewed as natural mechanisms or social forces, their existences mathematically and empirically beyond dispute; they are "social facts" (Durkheim (1958 [1895]), objectively real and unable to be wished away. Dannefer and Gannon (2005:4) have even asserted that Matthew effects and cumulative advantage processes in general are "a sufficiently pervasive, obdurate and irrepressible social tendency as to be considered a sociological law." Like the laws of gravity or natural selection, they do not care whether we like them or not, or even whether we are aware of them. And like Old Man River, they just keep rolling along.

Contrast the naturalist view with its main rival in the social sciences, commonly known as social constructionism or constructivism. In the constructionist view, social realities are not governed by immutable laws of nature over which we have no control. Rather, we create the social world through our choices, and what we have made, we can unmake. The practice of slavery, once justified as a natural and inevitable way of nature, is now generally viewed as an institution that human beings created and have largely chosen to abolish on moral and practical grounds. Similarly, constructionists would be inclined to see Matthew effects as consequences of the artificial rules of a social game that we have invented. These rules may result in extremely unequal outcomes, and like the rules of any game, they and their consequences can be changed.

Our own view lies somewhere between the extremes of naturalism and social constructionism. Matthew effects are observed in nature, and we human beings, as a part of—and not apart from—nature, are not entirely the authors of own circumstances. A natural tendency toward accelerating accumulations of advantage is apparent in each of the institutional spheres that we have considered thus far: the scientific, technological, economic, political, and educational. While some measure of inequality is no doubt inevitable, we may nonetheless choose to intervene in natural processes to exert a measure of restraint on the degree of cumulative advantage and inequality that is allowed to exist in human societies, just as we intervene to fight natural diseases or natural disasters. Whether or not we choose to intervene is a question of moral and political will.

In recent decades, the dominant view in the United States appears to have been that extreme inequalities are natural, normal, and even beneficial, and that not much can or should be done about them. But at other moments in American history, certain kinds or degrees of inequality were deemed unacceptable and were challenged in the public arena. The histories of the Civil War, the Progressive Era, the New Deal, and the civil rights movement offer abundant evidence that extreme forms of inequality can be confronted, counteracted, and contained through public opinion and public policy. In the wake of recent scandals involving the rapacity of financial elites, we may now be entering another such era.

SOCIAL BENEFITS AND COSTS OF MATTHEW EFFECTS

Few if any social scientists would deny that Matthew effects exist in social life, though some may doubt whether the concept leads us to unexpected discoveries. Elster (1990:134) remarks that the "Matthew effect owes its fame, I believe, more to the lucky choice of a phrase than to any surprising insights it has yielded." There is nothing terribly surprising about the existence of Matthew effects per se. It is commonly recognized in the clichés of our culture that the rich tend to get richer, that it takes money to make money, and that the big fish eat the little fish. Matthew effects in themselves are not especially controversial or unsettling, but their implications for ethics and public policy have people reaching for their swords.

How we view Matthew effects depends largely on how we view inequalities in general. Those who regard inequalities as natural, normal, and socially beneficial tend to emphasize the positive functions of inequality for the greater well-being of society. They are not particularly concerned with the moral implications of Matthew effects. Critics, on the other hand, tend to regard extreme inequalities as fundamentally unfair, unjust, and potentially destructive of social well-being. They focus on the negative functions of Matthew effects. Let us consider each of these perspectives in turn.

Among the most well-worn debates in modern sociology is the debate between functionalists and conflict theorists regarding the social functions of inequality. As noted in Chapter 1, Davis and Moore (1945) famously argued that unequal rewards are essential to the functioning of human societies. Where there are scarcities of personnel qualified to perform society's most vital functions, unequal rewards are needed to ensure that the best-qualified persons take on the burden of competently filling the most functionally important positions. Tumin (1953) strongly rebutted the Davis-Moore argument, responding that inegalitarian systems suppress the talent, arouse the hostility, and undermine the loyalty of the less advantaged; thus, the social consequences of inequality are largely dysfunctional.

Merton, though a functionalist, was fully cognizant of the potential dysfunctions and, in moral terms, the injustices that could result from inequalities generated by Matthew effects. Like Tumin, he was concerned about the "inadvertent suppression of talent" (1988:613). He noted that Matthew effects are largely unintended and unrecognized, and that one reason why such effects are not more widely recognized is that they are "at odds with certain interests and values of the society" (Merton 1988:615). Here he may have been referring to our national conceit that we live in a fundamentally fair society, and that people therefore deserve whatever advantages or disadvantages they happen to have. Merton, however, recognized that inequities produced by

Matthew effects are a social problem and not merely personal. Like C. Wright Mills (1959), he understood that the potentially destructive consequences of such social processes are not only the source of private troubles, but of public issues as well, requiring "new institutional arrangements for [their] reduction or elimination" (1988:615).

This is not to say that all Matthew effects are socially destructive or unjust in their consequences. The world is morally complex, and Matthew effects may have virtuous or vicious consequences or express elements of both. The accumulation of personal wealth, for example, may have mixed consequences depending upon how that wealth is gotten, how it is used, and how it affects the well-being of others. Wealth invested in productive and socially conscious enterprise may create meaningful work, useful products, and ripples of prosperity through the economy. Yet accumulated wealth in itself is not automatically beneficial in its social consequences, nor is it necessarily earned or deserved as a reward for moral virtue. If it were, saints would be rich and drug lords would be poor.

Matthew effects thus raise numerous ethical questions, though they seem to raise fewer such questions when one party's gain is not won at the expense of others. Consider the acquisition of reading skills. Your learning more vocabulary words does not prevent me from learning more words, and may even facilitate my learning if I learn new words from you. The learning of vocabulary is not a scarcity economy or a zero-sum game. One student's gain is not won at the expense of others. Thus, it is doubtful whether the common good is served by leveling down in areas such as education. Bast and Reitsma (1998:1388) suggest that "a better goal would be, of course, to lead the less able students to levels of (functional) reading skill that are minimally required in present-day society" without impeding the progress of better students. Bast and Reitsma are not expressing moral opposition to greater equality per se; they are merely advocating that such equality should be achieved by leveling up—that is, improving the performances of those who are falling behind rather than by holding the best students back.

In the economic sphere, where conditions of scarcity generally prevail, one party's gain is often another's loss, creating a zero-sum game.

In some instances, the gains of one party are won through exploiting another, as Marx and many others have long observed. In these instances we must ask for whom a given social arrangement is functional, for it is entirely possible that a social arrangement is functional for one social group and its interests, but profoundly dysfunctional for another (Stinchecombe 1968:91ff). This is especially true when conditions of scarcity rather than abundance prevail. One possible solution to this problem is to transform a zero-sum scarcity economy into a positive-sum abundance economy through economic growth, so that each party may enjoy a larger slice of a growing pie (Thurow 1980). Alternatively, the distribution of resources may be determined through class warfare, whether through parliamentary or violent means, with upper classes typically seeking to redistribute resources upward through the class system while lower classes seek redistribution downward.

EGALITARIAN AND INEGALITARIAN TRADITIONS

In the struggle over scarce and valued resources, we find widely varying conceptions of what constitutes distributive justice or the fair and equitable distribution of resources. Most would agree that the resources that individuals and groups enjoy should be, in some sense, fairly distributed and well deserved. Yet philosophical, religious, and ideological traditions differ regarding what constitutes a just distribution of resources. Some have condoned or defended extreme inequalities while others have opposed them.

Among philosophical traditions, the Aristotelian tradition in particular defends inequalities on the grounds that they are inscribed in the natural order of things. In his *Politics* and elsewhere, Aristotle (1987 [~340 BCE]), following Plato, articulated a vision of the good society as a hierarchical order in which the naturally superior rule the naturally inferior. Aristotle justified slavery on the grounds that those who are insufficiently rational are fitted by nature for nothing other than servitude. In medieval European thought, these ancient justifications of inequality were given a theological twist. Monarchs ruled their rigidly stratified societies by appeal to the doctrine of the divine right of kings, presenting themselves as the representatives of God on earth. Some forms of conservatism today, especially those with roots in ancient and medieval thought, still embrace an ideal of society in which clear hierarchies of human authority rest upon the higher authority of nature, or of nature's divine maker (Rigney 2001:94–97).

With the rise of modern capitalism, new philosophies have emerged to justify the extreme inequalities that market systems tend to generate. Libertarian descendants of the capitalist philosopher Adam Smith commonly argue that concentrations of wealth won in the marketplace are, by and large, earned and deserved. Modern libertarians and traditional conservatives, despite their philosophical differences and for rather different reasons, generally share a common hostility toward the ideal of social equality (Rigney 2001:94–95).

Arrayed against the inegalitarian traditions are various philosophical, religious, and ideological traditions emphasizing the value of greater social equality. Few if any of these traditions envision the possibility of total equality. Rather, they counsel restraints on the degree of social inequality that human societies should permit.[2] We find egalitarian themes, often alongside inegalitarian themes, in many of the world's major religious traditions (Smith 1991). Ancient Judaism, though set against a cultural backdrop of hierarchy and patriarchy, nonetheless upheld the egalitarian tradition of the sabbatical. Members of the community were expected to forgive debts and redistribute resources every seven years—and even more radically every seven-times-seven years, on the occasion of the Jubilee—in the interest of social justice. Christianity contains egalitarian themes as well. Jesus, in the Sermon on the Mount and throughout his teachings, expressed an ardent concern for the poor while simultaneously chastising the rich and urging an ethic of radical sharing. The egalitarian teachings of Jesus contrast sharply with the more hierarchical and conservative teachings of many of those who have come after him in church history (Lenski 1966:7–10; Wallis 2005). Egalitarian themes are evident in Islam as well, which teaches generosity toward the poor as one of its five essential pillars of faith. In Buddhism, the Mahayana ideal of the bodisattva, the compassionate Buddha, is a central theme. Each of these religious traditions, in its own distinctive way, teaches an ethic of sharing and greater equality.

Egalitarian themes have been prominent in numerous leftward political ideologies and social movements as well. The abolitionist and civil rights movements in American history have sought greater racial and ethnic equality. Trade-union movements have promoted greater equity in the wages and working conditions of labor. Feminists have sought parity in the economic and social status of women. Antipoverty and debt-relief movements have fought on behalf of persons and nations mired under crushing burdens of economic disadvantage. Each of these movements and their corresponding ideologies has advocated for redistributions of wealth and power from more to less advantaged segments of the population. Each has worked to create greater equality of opportunity and condition across class, race, gender, and nationality, rightly recognizing that equality of opportunity is impossible where there are extreme inequalities of condition and initial advantage.

In contemporary philosophy and ethics, relatively egalitarian traditions are represented by such figures as Peter Singer (1993; 2002) and John Rawls (1999). Singer argues that the world's extreme inequalities place a burden of moral responsibility on the privileged, demanding significant sacrifice on behalf of the well-being of the destitute and the desperately disadvantaged. Similarly, Rawls' influential *A Theory of Justice* proposes a thought experiment in which judgments about what is just or fair are made as though from behind an imaginary "veil of ignorance." Rawls asks what kind of society rational and self-interested individuals would design if they were hypothetically ignorant of their own social characteristics and locations (e.g, their sex, race, wealth, talents, etc.). This is akin to asking what kind of society we would construct now if we knew we would be randomly reincarnated into that society in the future. Rawls argues that in a just society, conceived through such a thought experiment, opportunities for human development would be more equally distributed than they are now. A fairer world would be a more egalitarian world.

The world as we find it now is, of course, profoundly unfair, despite wishful thinking to the contrary. Some are born into vast fortunes while others are born into famine. Some work hard all their lives and achieve little, while others inherit the opportunity to avoid work entirely. Disease and misfortune strike, without regard for the virtues of their victims. Wars, natural disasters and diseases kill innocents by the thousands and millions. Yet despite the obvious fact that life is not always fair, social psychologists have discovered a common phenomenon, which they call the belief in a just world (Lerner 1980). Many people are found to hold the strong belief, despite overwhelming evidence to the contrary, that the world is a just and fair place, and therefore, that people generally get what they deserve and deserve what they get. Lerner reports that people who subscribe to the just-world hypothesis are apt to attribute moral virtue to those who prosper and to blame victims for their own victimization. They are inclined to believe without evidence that lottery winners work harder and therefore are more deserving than those who have lost the lottery, or that women who are raped must have been "asking for it." Rubin and Peplau (1975) have found that those who embrace the just-world hypothesis tend to be more religious, more conservative, more authoritarian, and more negative in their attitudes toward the poor than those who do not. Andre and Velasquez (1990) argue that, by relieving the believer of responsibility for the well-being of others, belief in a just world rationalizes a lack of concern for actual justice.

A variation on the belief that the world is just is the widespread faith in American culture that the workings of a minimally regulated economic marketplace must be inherently fair and equitable in determining the distribution of rewards in society. According to a strong version of this belief, the market is viewed almost as an omniscient and infallible god (Cox 1999), meting out harsh justice by rewarding initiative and hard work while punishing sloth. To question the wisdom of the market is to blaspheme. Critics on the left deride this view as a kind of secular theology, or market fundamentalism, which naively associates economic advantage with moral virtue, presuming that those who have more must deserve what they have.

Generally, other things equal, market systems favor those who work harder and more inventively over those who do not. But other things are never equal. Many of the advantages people enjoy in life, whether biological, economic, or cultural, are inherited and unearned by those who enjoy them. Some advantages are gained virtuously, to be sure, but others are gained by the happenstance of being born into fortunate circumstances, or by living off the labor of others, or by deceit or force, or through sheer luck. Still others are gained through the self-amplifying accumulation of advantages conferred by Matthew effects. Such effects tend to amplify prior advantages and disadvantages irrespective of the moral virtue of their sources, further exacerbating inequities in the distribution of rewards.

Faith in the justice of markets is associated with a libertarian philosophy, the ethics of which emphasize the value of individualism, competition, personal liberty, and personal responsibility. More egalitarian ethical traditions, by contrast, tend to emphasize the need for a sense of social as well as personal responsibility, and hence the responsibility of each of us to help create a more fair and just world than the one we have found ourselves in. With regard to Matthew effects, egalitarians tend to argue that we have a responsibility to intervene and introduce countervailing forces to limit Matthew effects when such effects produce dramatically unfair results.

COUNTERVAILING FORCES

As noted previously, Merton recognized that Matthew effects may have destructive as well as constructive consequences. He alluded to the need for "new institutional arrangements" to reduce or eliminate such adverse effects when they arise (1988:615), recognizing early on (1942) that a democratic society must introduce new forms of organization "to preserve and extend equality of opportunity" to "put democratic values into practice" (1973 [1942]:273). He gave the name "countervailing processes" (1988:617–19) to those forces that restrain Matthew effects. While he did not elaborate upon these processes in detail, we can identify several such countervailing forces, both natural and artificial. Let us consider several of these.

MATHEMATICAL FORCES

Nothing in nature grows forever; even exponential growth curves must slow eventually as they approach an asymptotic limit. Thus, even the most successful individuals or groups must encounter limits to the growth of advantage. We have observed how the mathematics of compound interest can produce and sustain Matthew effects. Yet there are also mathematical or statistical principles that work in the opposite direction to limit or even reverse such effects—to limit advantage, and hence, to make greater equality possible. Consider the principle of regression toward the mean, the statistical phenomenon wherein, in repeated measures of a given characteristic over time, extreme initial scores are followed by scores that tend increasingly toward the average. We might expect that the offspring of two geniuses, or two superb athletes, will also be geniuses or super-athletes. What we observe, however, is that their offspring are likely to be closer to average than either parent. Regression toward the mean tends to mute extreme inequalities over time, working in the opposite direction of Matthew effects. Thus Shaywitz, Holford, Holahan, Fletcher, Stuebing, Francis, and Shaywitz (1995:899) finds that "potential demonstration of a Matthew effect [in reading abilities] is confounded by regression toward the mean. Regression effects occur because children with unusually high (low) scores on one testing will tend to score lower (higher) on the next test by pure chance, even if no real change in ability has taken place in the meantime." Shaywitz and his colleagues conclude that "even in the case of IQ scores, where a Matthew effect is apparent, regression to the mean overwhelms the relatively small Matthew effect" (1995:905).

Another statistical principle that mitigates extreme inequalities is the ceiling effect, together with its counterpart, the floor effect. Ceiling and floor effects occur when statistical scores cannot go beyond a given upper or lower limit. The percentage of computer users in a given population cannot go above 100 percent or below 0 percent. As noted in Chapter 2, increases in the percentages of computer users in advanced industrial societies, such as the United States, inevitably must slow down as the figure for users approaches the asymptotic limit of 100 percent. Countries in the developing world, by contrast, may still dramatically improve their percentages because they have more room to grow. The result is that, as developed countries approach the ceiling of computer usage, developing countries may continue to grow and catch up, steadily reducing the inequality between themselves and developed countries.

To offer another example, in academic grades, A students are not likely to widen the gap between themselves and C students because there is no grade higher than an A. They have reached the ceiling and have nowhere else to go. Meanwhile, C students can continue to improve, narrowing the gap between themselves and those at the top.

A third statistical phenomenon, which we may call intergenerational dispersion, occurs when the advantages of one generation are distributed among the multiple members of the next (Keister 2005:128–34). Consider the bequest of wealth from a benefactor to a more numerous group of beneficiaries. In such instances, the dispersion of inheritance results in a redistribution among households, which has the overall effect of reducing inequality.[3] Thus, if I divide my purely imaginary fortune of $1 million among five households, each household will receive $200,000: a deconcentration of wealth. Keister (2005:128–34) observes that this dilution of resources increases with the number of siblings. As siblings receive their shares of the previous generation's fortunes, and as they later divide these fortunes among their own beneficiaries, wealth gradually becomes less concentrated, creating greater equality among households. Of course, other economic forces, such as compound interest, are simultaneously at play to reconcentrate wealth. Therefore, intergenerational dispersion alone does not determine future structures of inequality.

A final statistical (and economic) phenomenon to be considered is the trickle-down effect. While conservative economists often object to the term (e.g., Sowell 2004:188–89), the trickle-down effect is said to result from policies that reduce taxes or otherwise benefit upper-income groups for the purpose of stimulating economic growth. Such policies have the immediate effect of further concentrating economic advantage at the top, but hypothetically benefit the less advantaged if untaxed monies are invested productively, creating new jobs and thus gradually dispersing prosperity to those below. Skeptics note, however, that in reality, few such benefits reach the bottom. In the wake of the Reagan tax cuts of the 1980s, 60 percent of economic benefits flowed to the richest 1 percent of the population, with little trickling down to middle-income groups and even less to lower-income groups (Nasar 1992). Alternative proposals to reduce the taxes of middle- and lower-income groups, thereby increasing consumer spending and creating a trickle-up or wick-up effect, have received less consideration from policy makers in recent years.[4]

THE VICISSITUDES OF COMPETITION

Beyond statistical factors, there are also social factors that counteract Matthew effects. In competitive systems with limited resources, there is only so much room at the top, whether in science (Merton 1988:608), athletics, or commerce. Competitive systems, such as commercial markets or athletic leagues, may either promote or undermine Matthew effects, depending on how the competition is structured and regulated. On the one hand, market systems often tend to create self-perpetuating monopolies and oligopolies in the absence of countervailing regulation. In these instances, dominant firms exercise economic and political power to crush competitors and amplify their own advantages; the comparable phenomenon in athletic leagues is that of the perennial dynasty. On the other hand, when regulations are set in place to protect and invigorate competition—as when legislatures enact fair trade policies, or when the National Football League decides to introduce rules creating greater parity among professional football teams, as it did some years ago—dominant firms and franchises can be toppled and upstarts can more readily rise to the top.

Schumpeter (1942) famously described capitalism as a system of creative destruction. Competitive economies can be extremely unstable, and no firm's success is safe as long as others are competing aggressively for dominance. This is true for several reasons. Veblen (1915) noted long ago that early innovators in an industry frequently pay the "penalty of the taking the lead." The leading firm or nation in a given industry may dominate for a time, but competing firms and nations can learn from its mistakes, improve upon its products, and surpass it. Thus Microsoft is keenly aware that it cannot afford to rest on its laurels, lest it be overtaken by nimbler and more innovative competitors, just as IBM was previously overtaken by other computer firms. In very competitive systems, the rich do not get richer forever. They rise and fall as other firms or nations rise to take their places. Current anxieties over global economic competition reflect the growing recognition among many Americans that U.S. dominance of the world economy since World War II is in jeopardy, and that the economic dynasties of the future might be Chinese or Indian (Friedman 2000; 2005). Rostow (1980) seems to have anticipated the rise of China and India in the world system when he wrote *Why the Poor Get Richer and the Rich Slow Down.*

Consider as well the famous aphorism that a fool and his money are soon parted. No amount of initial advantage can save an individual, firm, or nation from the peril of disastrous errors in judgment and incompetent decisions. As noted in Chapter 2, some are "wrecked by success," as Freud put it. The Matthew effect is no insurance against the feckless squandering of advantage.

EGALITARIAN SOCIAL MOVEMENTS

Major social movements throughout history, from the slave rebellions of ancient Rome and the peasant rebellions of the Middle Ages through the French Revolution and into the present day, have risen to challenge the privileges of accumulated advantage. We have previously noted several such movements in American history, including abolitionism, the Progressive movement, the New Deal, and the modern labor, civil rights, and feminist movements, each rising in its turn. Such egalitarian movements do not succeed in the long run, however, unless they institutionalize their opposition to inequality, especially through the agency of government and law.

GOVERNMENTAL INTERVENTION

Governments often have been essential in counteracting Matthew effects that are deemed to be socially destructive. Examples of countervailing legislation are fairly numerous and obvious. In American history, these have included progressive taxation, estate taxation, transfer payments of various sorts (e.g., food stamps, housing subsidies), affirmative action laws, Project Head Start, minority set-asides, and a host of other measures and programs aimed at redistributing resources and opportunities to disadvantaged persons and groups. Such programs have had some success. Hernandez and Macartney (2008) report that black and Hispanic children have made significant advances on a composite of twenty-eight indicators of health and well-being over the past twenty years, narrowing their overall gap relative to white non-Hispanic children. These gains are attributed in part to governmental programs providing disadvantaged families with subsidized child care and preschool education, child health insurance, and earned-income tax credits (Hernandez and Macartney 2008; Koch 2008). Similarly, No Child Left Behind laws, despite their defects, may help to explain narrowing gaps in black and Hispanic performance relative to white non-Hispanic students, with improvement among all groups on reading and mathematics tests (National Assessment of Educational Programs 2005). Meanwhile, the wage gap between men and women in the United States has continued to narrow since the 1980s (Leonhardt 2003), a trend that would be difficult to account for without citing governmental legislation promoting equal employment opportunities for women.

Conservative critics typically argue that governmental programs designed to achieve greater equality often unintentionally do more harm than good. Such arguments, whatever their merits, usually neglect to ask where the United States would be as a nation if concentrations of accumulated advantage had been allowed to grow unimpeded—if there had been no progressive taxation, no Social Security or Medicare, no civil rights movement, no equal rights movement for women. While governmental intervention in these instances has been no panacea, efforts to roll back progressive income and estate taxation and civil rights protections, if implemented, would almost certainly have negative consequences of their own, further widening the vast chasm that separates the advantaged from the disadvantaged in American society.

The challenges of globalization also threaten to exacerbate inequalities in the United States. Friedman (2000; 2005) has called for the expansion of governmental programs in response to increasing global economic competition and uncertainty. He has proposed a range of "trapezes," "trampolines," and "safety nets" that would help American workers to survive and rebound from the economic dislocations and instabilities of the world economy through such measures as job retraining and lifelong education. The economic and social costs of investing in such programs must be weighed against the cost of doing nothing.

ALTRUISM AND ENLIGHTENED SELF-INTEREST

One final brake on Matthew effects deserves special mention. It sometimes happens that those with large advantages choose, whether from true altruism or from enlightened self-interest, to act in ways that redistribute benefits to the less advantaged. The distinction between altruism and enlightened self-interest is important, for the two are commonly confounded. Altruism, in the words of St. Paul, "gives and doesn't count the cost." True altruism is genuinely self-sacrificial. Enlightened self-interest, though admirable, weighs the likelihood that an act of generosity redounds to the benefit of the giver. In deciding to price his cars attractively and pay his workers well enough to afford them, Henry Ford was not acting so much from a concern for the well-being of his employees as from a concern for the well-being of his eventual profit statements. Even if it did not emanate from a spirit of self-sacrifice, however, this shrewd business decision raised the general prosperity of the working classes and helped to create a larger middle class in the process.

But what are we to make of philanthropists? Are they true altruists? When billionaires Bill Gates and Warren Buffet donated a substantial part of their fortunes toward eradicating childhood diseases in developing countries, was this primarily for the sake of tax and public relations advantages, or to amass greater self-esteem and social honor, as some claim? Or were these benefactors acting from an authentic concern for the well-being of others? Whatever complex combination of motives may have been at play in their decisions, their philanthropy has inarguably resulted in some redistribution of accumulated advantage to the severely disadvantaged, countering prior Matthew effects that helped them to accumulate their vast wealth in the first place.

CONCLUSION: THE GOOSE AND THE GOLDEN EGG

Despite the occasional act of philanthropy, it seems unlikely that our age will be remembered as an age of altruism. Business writer Robert Samuelson (2001) captures something of the spirit of our times in an essay announcing that "Americans care less about the gap between the rich and the poor than about just getting ahead" and suggests that this is as it should be. Here the cynic is tempted to conclude on a bitter note. Privileged individuals and strata, in the United States and around the world, continue to enjoy large and growing advantages. These advantages are not entirely—or perhaps even primarily—the result of their own hard work, ingenuity, or moral virtue, but are rather largely the result of the sociology and mathematics of the Matthew effect amplifying prior advantages, whether biological, economic, or cultural. It is as though the privileged are riding the crest of an impersonal wave, not of their own making, but from which they benefit nonetheless, while others less fortunate are dragged beneath the wave in its undertow. To the degree that Matthew effects amplify prior advantages and disadvantages, both the fortunes of the fortunate and the misfortunes of the unfortunate are unearned and undeserved (Gladwell 2008:15–34).

The cynic continues: The advantaged fervently wish to believe that their advantages are earned and well deserved. Self-interest is a powerful force in human affairs, shaping our ideologies and our perceptions of reality. Thus, the advantaged tend to embrace ideologies—such as the cherished myth of a just world—that justify not only the products of Matthew effects but, more important, the processes or mechanisms that produce them. Those who benefit from Matthew effects strive to protect not only their golden eggs, but also the goose that laid them. Precisely because they have accumulated large social advantages, they are well positioned to defend these interests successfully, and even to expand them further through the self-serving, self-perpetuating, and self-amplifying exercise of economic, political, and cultural power. Thus the advantaged generally succeed in resisting attempts to temper or counterbalance Matthew effects through egalitarian initiatives. They employ their cumulative advantages to protect the Matthew effects that allow them to accumulate still more advantages. The cynic concludes that this is the way of the world, and not much can be done about it.

Yet there is something in this cynical conclusion that offends our sense of fairness. The cynic seems to accept too easily the inevitability of a world of inherited privilege, amplified advantage, and extreme and widening inequalities. Have we no moral or social responsibility to render the world a fairer place?

How might those who stand in democratic and egalitarian moral traditions respond to the cynic's analysis? They might begin by noting that history often takes unexpected twists and turns. Periods of growing inequality in American history have often met unanticipated resistance from countervailing forces, and social movements from abolitionism through the Progressive movement, the New Deal, and the civil rights and feminist movements to the present day have always arisen to challenge extreme inequities. New ideas, leadership, and constellations of interest and potential alliance continually emerge and coalesce. In the future, it is almost certain that resistance against extreme inequalities will be not just national, but international in scope. We do not yet know from what unexpected directions such resistance may arise. But we do know this: A wider awareness of Matthew effects and their potentially destructive and constructive consequences can raise the quality of public discussion to a higher level among social scientists, policy makers, and citizens at large, informing our choices and our actions as we continue to confront the vast inequities of the twenty-first century.

APPENDIX

TRENDS IN ECONOMIC INEQUALITY

AT THE END of chapter 3, we asked whether public policies in modern democracies, such as the United States, have succeeded in producing more equitable distributions of wealth and income over time, as Gunnar Myrdal had hoped they would, and whether the world as a whole has become more egalitarian in the distribution of its economic resources. These are complicated and difficult questions, and their answers depend largely on how we choose to define and measure inequality. This appendix looks at these questions in greater detail, examining trends in inequality in both the United States and the world at large.

IS THERE GROWING ECONOMIC INEQUALITY IN THE UNITED STATES?

Before attempting to answer these questions, we must consider the array of alternative ways to conceptualize and measure inequality. Anyone looking for simple answers to questions about trends in inequality soon encounters a bewildering range of methodological questions, such as the following:

1. Should we focus on inequalities of income, whether expressed in units of time, such as weekly or annually, or of wealth, accumu-

lated over time? Economists find that, in general, wealth is far more unequally distributed than income.

2. Which units of analysis should we compare? Should we compare individuals? Households? Nations? World regions?

3. Which statistical measures of inequality should we employ? Should we track changes in the ratios of total wealth or income controlled by the richest and poorest segments of the population (e.g., by the top and bottom deciles)? Or should we focus on statistics such as the Gini coefficient and the Theil index, which summarize trends across the entire distribution of income or wealth, and not just at the extremes? Patterns of inequality may vary according to which methods we employ, and many such measures are available.[1]

4. Which time intervals should we examine? Should we consider trends over five years? Twenty-five years? Centuries? These choices are frequently determined by the availability of data, but in any case, the length of the time series we examine can bear significantly on our discernment and interpretation of trends.

5. How trustworthy is the quality of the economic data we examine (Firebaugh 2003:52–57)? Are data constructed in the same way from one country to the next? Are economic statistics themselves subject to political manipulation (Alonso and Starr 1987; Jencks 1987)?

By almost any measure we care to examine, economic inequalities in the United States have tended to widen substantially in recent decades. Since the late 1970s in the United States, the most advantaged have grown vastly richer on a scale that even the magnates of the Gilded Age of the 1890s could not have imagined, while disadvantaged groups have stagnated or even lost ground. Observers on the left (e.g., Braun 1997; Collins, Leondar-Wright, and Sklar 1999; Phillips 2002; Wolff 1995/2002) have viewed these statistical trends with alarm and sought to lay much of the blame on the conservative economic policies of the Reagan administration during the 1980s, echoed in the policies of the second Bush administration after 2001. Conservative defenders of these policies (e.g., Cox and Alm 1999, Sowell 2004) have argued that such policies stimulate economic growth, eventually benefiting all segments of the population. Other factors contributing to the widening gap between rich and poor, including the decline of organized labor, the rise of new technologies, and increasing international trade competition, will be considered further on.

There has not always been increasing economic polarization in American history. In previous eras, we have seen varied patterns in the relations among the rich, the poor, and those in the middle. In *Wealth and Democracy*, Phillips (2002) analyzes the history of inequality in the United States, identifying ebbs and flows in the distribution of economic resources. He notes that our own time resembles, in many respects, the industrial expansion of the late nineteenth century. During this Gilded Age, the captains of finance and industry (whom Mark Twain called the "robber barons") accumulated vast fortunes, often through ruthless means. It was not for nothing that this era was characterized as an age of social Darwinism (Hofstadter 1992). Fierce competition and increasing concentrations of wealth in the hands of the few eventually provoked a progressive counterreaction.

During the Progressive Era of the early twentieth century, Theodore Roosevelt's proposal to establish a graduated or progressive income tax, later enacted into law under Woodrow Wilson, placed a larger share of the tax burden on the shoulders of those who could most afford to pay. The graduated or progressive income tax was just one of several Progressive measures designed to redress the extreme inequalities of wealth that had accumulated during the Gilded Age. Progressive tax policies tended to benefit the middle and lower classes at the expense of the upper classes. Here was an instance of the Matthew effect being countervailed.

During the Great Depression, rich and poor alike suffered severe economic losses. In this period, the rich and poor grew poorer simultaneously. With the postwar recovery, however, the United States entered a period of sustained economic growth that benefited lower, middle, and upper classes alike. During the Eisenhower, Kennedy, and Johnson eras, the rich and the poor grew richer together. Labor unions were much stronger than they are today, and large corporations had not yet moved manufacturing operations abroad en masse to take advantage of cheap international labor. Phillips (2002:76, 137) calls this postwar era of shared prosperity the Great Compression, because the gap between rich and poor diminished.

By the 1970s, shared prosperity had given way once again to an era of growing inequality that continues to this day. Lowenstein (2007) examines a 2004 Congressional Budget Office analysis reporting that, while incomes in the poorest quintile of U.S. households since 1979 grew by only 2 percent (adjusted for inflation), those in the middle quintile grew by 15 percent and those in the top quintile by a whopping 63 percent. Thus, while there has been substantial economic growth in recent decades, the benefits of that growth have tended to rise like cream to the top of the American class system. Lowenstein notes that most of the meager improvement at the bottom has been due to longer working hours rather than higher wages. Meanwhile, the upper 1 percent of households captured 16 percent of total income in 2004, up from 9 percent in 1979. Though it is often said that a rising tide lifts all boats, former labor secretary Robert Reich quips that "the rising tide is lifting all yachts" (in Bai 2007:70), potentially igniting a populist backlash from below.

That the rich do not always get richer and the poor poorer does not necessarily signify the absence of Matthew effects. Rather, other forces—countervailing forces, such as progressive taxation or the existence of strong labor unions—may have sometimes counterbalanced and neutralized the natural tendency of the advantaged to become more advantaged. Many forces are at work in the world at any given time, and the Matthew effect is only one of them.

Economists Emmanuel Saez and Thomas Piketty (Piketty and Saez 2003; Saez 2005) have undertaken careful analyses of nearly a century of trends in income distribution in the United States. Their findings corroborate Phillips' more qualitative analysis of ebbs and flows in income inequality over time. The authors find a clear U-shaped pattern in the proportion of income received by the top decile and percentile of earners from the early twentieth century to the present. Inequalities were most extreme in the 1920s, dropped dramatically during World War II, but regained their earlier heights by the beginning of the twenty-first century. Paul Ryscavage (1999) has done a similar analysis and has reached similar findings. Ryscavage reports that the Gini coefficient reflecting income inequality for families stood at nearly .55 (on a 0–1 scale) during the 1920s, but then fell sharply during the Great Depression and continued to decline during and after World War II, stabilizing at just over .35 during the 1950s and 1960s. Family income inequality began to creep up again in the 1970s, however, accelerating in the 1980s and continuing to rise to .45 by the mid-1990s (1999:156, 180).

Economists have sought to uncover the underlying mechanisms that generate these growing inequalities. In one classic study, Simon Kuznets (1955) identified technological innovation as an important source of inequality. He observed that national inequalities tend to increase in the early stages of industrialization as new technologies create new but unevenly distributed wealth. The transition from a relatively low-income agricultural economy to a more lucrative industrial economy benefits those who enter the industrial sector. As increasing numbers of workers enter the urban-industrial economy over time, however, inequalities begin to decline. Piketty and Saez (2003:2) suggest that, in keeping with Kuznet's hypothesis, we may now be in the early stages of a "new industrial revolution . . . leading to increasing inequality [which] will decline at some point, as more and more workers benefit from the innovations."

While Piketty and Saez acknowledge the importance of technology, they also emphasize the role of tax policy, and public policy generally, as a mechanism for modulating inequality. Changes in the degree of inequality in the United States have tended to coincide with changes in the tax code. Taxes during World War II were sharply progressive, corresponding to a period of shared sacrifice and growing economic equality in the United States. However, the decline in income tax progressivity since the Reagan era of the 1980s has tended to produce levels of inequality not seen in nearly a century (Piketty and Saez 2003:24).

Autor, Katz, and Kearney (2008) have identified a third mechanism affecting the distribution of income: They observe that market forces, responding largely to changes in technology, have caused changes in the demand for both high-paying and low-paying skills. In the 1990s, market forces expanded opportunities for employment in both high-

skill, high-paid occupations and low-skill, low-paid occupations, resulting in a divergence of upper-tail and lower-tail wage inequality
and creating a growing polarization of income in the United States.
Strong growth in the demand for educated workers has outrun supply in recent decades, creating widening wage differentials in what
Goldin and Katz (2008) describe as a "race between education and
technology." Some have argued that an influx of immigrant labor, especially from Latin America, has affected low-end wages significantly,
though evidence suggests that the effects of higher immigration on
labor markets is actually relatively small (Butcher and Card 1991).

Economic and social analysts have proposed a multitude of other
possible mechanisms underlying the trend toward greater inequality in the United States since the 1970s (Cassady 1995; Ryscavage
1999:109–30, 185). Among these are the deindustrialization of the
economy and the attendant growth of relatively lower-paying jobs
in the service sector (Bluestone and Harrison 1982; Firebaugh 2003);
growing international trade competition and the outsourcing of jobs
to lower-wage countries; changes in family composition, such as those
resulting from high divorce rates and out-of-wedlock births, creating
a larger proportion of financially vulnerable single-parent families;
and the erosion of the minimum wage. These and other factors interact with each other in complex and poorly understood ways to produce shifting patterns of inequality. Ryscavage emphasizes that there
are no simple explanations for these patterns. No single factor alone
accounts for the growth of inequality.

According to Ryscavage (1999:157–58), most studies of inequality find that incomes and earnings are more unequally distributed in
the United States than they are in other industrialized nations. And
while other industrialized countries have also experienced increasing
income inequality in recent years, Ryscavage notes that the United
States has shown the sharpest increases in the modern world.

Thus far, we have focused our attention on trends in income inequality. Patterns of inequality appear far more pronounced, however,
when we shift our focus from income to wealth, or accumulated assets, as wealth tends to be far more unequally distributed than income. While data on the distribution of wealth through time are hard-

er to find than income data, the evidence suggests a similar pattern of increasing economic concentration in the United States in recent decades (Keister 2000; Wolff 1995/2002). Wolff (2002:28–29) reports that, by the end of the twentieth century, the top 1 percent of the U.S. population had managed to accumulate more than 40 percent of all stock, and the top 20 percent owned well over 80 percent. Meanwhile, the bottom 40 percent of the population controlled less than 5 percent of total wealth, and nearly one in five households actually had a negative net worth (Collins, Leondar-Wright, and Sklar 1999:6–10), with debts (including mortgage) exceeding total assets. More recently, the Federal Reserve Board, reporting the results of the Survey of Consumer Finances (SCF) over time, finds that the share of total net assets controlled by the richest 1 percent of Americans has increased from 30.1 percent in 1989 to nearly 34 percent in 2007 (Kennickell 2009:Table 4a).

Inequalities of wealth intensified in the early twenty-first century as federal income tax cuts favoring the upper classes further concentrated assets at the pinnacle of American society, causing the super-rich to pull increasingly away from the merely rich (Johnston 2005). Paradoxically, public opinion favored these tax cuts even as people expressed concern over growing economic inequalities, and as the lives of the less advantaged became increasingly precarious (Frank 2005:1–10; McMahon and TeSelle 2004). Recent evidence suggests that these inequalities are continuing to accelerate (Johnston 2007).

Observers on the left have seen in these trends an ominous drift toward declining rates of mobility and the gradual formation of a caste-like system of inherited privilege in the United States (e.g., Krugman 2004).[2] Observers on the right have painted a sunnier picture. Cox and Alm's (1999) *Myths of Rich and Poor* describes itself as a "good news book." While the authors acknowledge and even celebrate that the rich in the United States have grown dramatically richer in recent decades, they present evidence that the poor, on the whole, have been getting richer too. Thanks to the marvels of modern technology, rich and poor alike enjoy a much higher standard of living than the kings and queens of yore, with access to amenities that were not previously available even to the most fortunate.

Cox and Alm present data from the University of Michigan's Panel Survey on Income Dynamics to demonstrate that poverty in the United States, in contrast to the much deeper poverty that prevails in many developing countries, is largely a function of age (1999:205; see also Cauchon 2007).[3] Young adults may earn low incomes early in their working lives, and are therefore overrepresented among the poor, but their earnings tend to increase steadily with age and experience. Few stay in the lowest income quintile forever. Poverty, Cox and Alm argue, is usually a transitory experience, and there are ample opportunities to rise above it for those willing to work hard. Meanwhile, the economic status of women and minorities continues to improve, they note, further undermining the left-populist image of a nation severely divided between haves and have-nots (1999:69–89).

Which of these competing visions of American life are we to believe? Each is selective in its choice and presentation of facts. Conservatives Cox and Alm prefer to discuss income inequality rather than the far more unequal distribution of wealth. They also choose to focus on the mobility of households within a single generation (i.e., from young adulthood to retirement), rather than between generations, for which data show dramatically higher degrees of inequality and lower rates of social mobility among economic strata from one generation to the next (e.g., Keister 2005:57). Cox and Alm feature statistics that obscure stark economic contrasts among strata, while observers on the left tend to do the opposite. Analysts on the left often cite real declines in average hourly wages in the United States since the early 1970s as evidence of workers' growing misery. Those on the right insist that the consumer price index used to calculate these figures overstates inflation by more than 1 percent per year. If hourly wages were adjusted for the true inflation rate, they insist, the apparent decline would become an increase (Cox and Alm 1999:5, 20–21). Whatever the relative merits of these contending positions may be, it is fair to say that statistics are often constructed, presented, and interpreted with political and economic interests in mind, and that both the left and the right frequently indulge in what Alonso and Starr (1987) have called the politics of numbers.

The left and right continue to disagree over whether middle- and lower-income groups in the United States have advanced, stagnated, or declined in recent years. Once again, much depends on our choice of methods and measures. There is little disagreement, however, about the success of the successful. By virtually any measure, the rich in recent decades have grown substantially richer in what economists Frank and Cook (1996) have termed the winner-take-all society, leaving the rest of American society further and further behind.

IS THERE GROWING ECONOMIC INEQUALITY AROUND THE WORLD?

Turning our attention from the United States to the world at large, what patterns and trends in economic inequality do we observe? Myrdal was hopeful that democratic political institutions in developed societies could check market forces and prevent extreme inequalities from arising within those countries. But he was less optimistic at the international level: He observed that advanced industrial nations tend to dominate poorer nations through the extraction of natural resources, exploitation of cheap labor, and expansion of new markets for manufactured goods. He noted that the misery of poorer nations is further compounded by problems of overpopulation and capital flight in the investments of their own upper classes. Here Mydal's analysis converges at several points with those of world systems and dependency theorists (e.g., Cardoso and Faletto 1979; Frank 1993; Wallerstein 1976/1980), particularly in their shared emphasis on the lopsided advantages that nations at the center of the world economy enjoy at the expense of those on the periphery.[4] Attributing many of these inequities to colonialism, Myrdal held out hope that postcolonial movements of national independence, together with more egalitarian policy initiatives from international organizations, such as the United Nations, might begin to redress the extreme economic inequalities that had opened up between richer and poorer nations. But he maintained that market forces in an increasingly globalized economy would only tend to reinforce and amplify global inequalities.

Have Myrdal's prophesies come to pass? Have free trade and the globalization of world markets in fact resulted in rich nations growing richer as poor nations have grown poorer? Or is globalization "flattening" the world (Friedman 2005), leading toward a greater equalization in the distribution of economic resources? This question is at the heart of current controversies surrounding globalization, and once again the answer seems to depend largely on how we ask the question and on what methods we use to resolve it.[5]

To begin to appreciate the complexities of the question, consider the data in the table below, adapted from the Human Development Report issued by the United Nations Development Programme (2002). This table compares changes in the gross domestic product (GDP) of seven regions of the world from 1975 to 2000. Do these data offer evidence for or against the existence of Matthew effects in the global distribution of income? The evidence, as it turns out, is ambiguous.

GLOBAL DISPARITIES IN INCOME, 1975–2000
GDP PER CAPITA (2000 PURCHASING POWER PARITY, THOUSANDS OF U.S. DOLLARS)

| | GDP PER CAPITA | | | PERCENT CHANGE |
	1975	1990	2000	1975–2000
East Asia	1.0	2.2	4.5	+350
South Asia	1.4	1.8	2.4	+71
Sub-Saharan Africa	2.4	2.1	2.0	−17
Arab states	3.2	4.0	4.5	+41
Latin America and Caribbean	5.8	6.2	7.3	+26
Central and Eastern Europe and Commonwealth of Independent States	n.a.	9.3	6.9	−26*
High-income OECD	16.0	23.3	27.8	+74
World	5.2	6.8	8.0	+54

Note: *1990–2000 only. n.a. = not available. OECD = Organization for Economic Cooperation and Development.

Source: Estimates are adapted from a report of the UN Development Programme (2002:19) based on World Bank data (2002). For some conceptual and methodological criticisms of the UN report, including its use of nations rather than individuals as its unit of analysis, see Postrel (2002).

If we compare percent increases in per capita GDP by region over a twenty-five-year period, we find that some regions—most notably East Asia, including China—have experienced phenomenal economic growth of 350 percent over this period. Other regions, including the high-income members of the Organization for Economic Cooperation and Development (OECD)—essentially the nations of Western Europe, the United States, Canada, Japan, Australia, and New Zealand—and South Asia (principally India) have also grown robustly, at 74 percent and 71 percent, respectively, during this period. Latin American and Arab states have grown at slower rates, while sub-Saharan Africa has actually experienced negative growth (–17 percent) over the same period, as have Central and Eastern Europe (including the Russian Federation), declining by 26 percent since 1990, if the latter data are valid.[6]

Do these data tend to confirm or disconfirm the existence of global Matthew effects? Are the rich nations of the world getting richer as the poor grow poorer? Looking only at percent increases in per capita GDP reveals a mixed picture. While high-income OECD countries continue to enjoy robust growth rates, the economies of East Asia are growing at a dramatically faster rate, suggesting that while the rich economies are getting richer, some poor economies are getting richer as well, and more quickly. If this trend continued for many decades, East Asia could eventually catch and surpass the OECD countries. The economy of India, following economic reforms in the 1990s, also is growing rapidly, at rates that exceed those of the OECD countries. The Matthew effect hypothesis is disconfirmed in this instance. However, South Asia (apart from India) and the Arab states show rates of growth that are positive, yet lower than those in the high-income OECD countries—a kind of relative Matthew effect, whereby the rich get richer while the poor also get richer, but at a slower rate. Finally, consider the plight of Central and Eastern Europe and, more tragically, sub-Saharan Africa, the negative growth rates of which cause them to fall further behind the OECD countries, not just in relative but in absolute terms. As the rich countries grow both relatively and absolutely richer, many poor (African) and middle-income (Central and Eastern European) countries have grown relatively or even absolutely poorer.

Matthew effects become more apparent when we examine not only comparative growth rates, but also absolute economic gaps between richer and poorer countries, expressed in purchasing power parity (PPP) U.S. dollars. Here we find that from 1975 to 2000, average GDP in the richest countries increased by about $11,800 per capita, compared with $3,500 in East Asia, $1,500 in Latin America, $1,300 in the Arab states, and $1,000 in South Asia. Eastern Europe suffered a $2,400 decline per capita following the collapse of Soviet communism according to these data, while per capita income in the destitute economies of sub-Saharan Africa declined by $400 between 1975 and 2000. Thus, if we contrast the richest regions of the world (including the United States) with the poorest (sub-Saharan Africa), there is no doubt that the gap between the richest and poorest countries of the world has widened dramatically in recent decades, both relatively and absolutely.

Whether globalization primarily accounts for the widening gap between richer and poorer nations, however, is not at all clear. Those countries that currently display the most impressive economic advances (e.g., China and India) are doing so largely through their growing participation in world markets. On the other hand, the countries that lag farthest behind (especially those in Africa) are generally those least integrated into the global economy.

Yet the integration of nations and regions into the global economy does not in itself guarantee prosperity. Even staunch defenders of globalization, such as Thomas Friedman (2000; 2005), acknowledge that global economic competition often has brutal consequences for nations and individuals who lack the resources to compete effectively in the Darwinian struggle for global economic survival. To his credit, Friedman does not sugarcoat the increasing competitiveness of the world economy. While the leveling of the field certainly produces winners (including growing middle classes in China and India) and generates unimagined wealth for a few at the top of the world system, it leaves others hopelessly behind, opening an ever-widening chasm between the world's most and least advantaged people and nations.

In this new social Darwinism, the future belongs to the swift and adaptable. Friedman chooses a suitably Darwinian metaphor to drive his point home, telling his famous story of the lion and the gazelle (2000:331). Each goes to bed at night knowing that it must outrun the other or die. Both know that "when the sun comes up, they had better start running." So it is with the struggle for economic survival, Friedman warns, and unfortunately, not everyone is equipped to survive the race. In Friedman's parlance, some nations are "lions," while others are "turtles" or "wounded gazelles." Friedman fears a backlash from the losers of this ruthless competition, who are not convinced that current forms of globalization are either desirable or inevitable (2000:327–47).

Most laypersons would interpret the widening gap among nations and regions as evidence of growing inequality in the world. It may surprise many readers to learn that this is not what economists usually mean when they speak of inequality. Herein lies a key to understanding why research studies often seem to contradict each other concerning whether global inequalities are increasing or decreasing. Why does the Human Development Report find increasing inequalities (as shown in the table above) while others studies (e.g., Bhalla 2002; Firebaugh 2003; Sala-i-Martin 2002) announce that, contrary to popular perception, global income inequalities are in fact declining?

The mystery is partially solved when we realize that lay people and economists tend to use the term *inequality* in rather different ways. Lay people suppose that if those at the high end of an economic distribution are getting richer and those at the lower end are getting poorer, the gap between the two is widening and, therefore, inequality is growing. Economists, on the other hand, have a mathematical concept of economic inequality as any departure from a perfectly uniform distribution of wealth or income, which considers not only what is happening at either end of the economic spectrum, but also what is happening between the extremes. If the richest are gaining and the poorest are falling farther behind, the economist's measures of inequality (e.g., Lorenz curves and their derivative Gini coefficients) might still show declining overall inequality if intermediate segments of the distribution are advancing sufficiently. The Gini coefficient and similar indices attempt to boil this overall pattern down to a single number (ranging from 0 = perfect equality to 1 = perfect inequality), and if this number shows declines over time, then inequalities are said to be diminishing, even if the richest countries are becoming absolutely richer while the poorest become absolutely poorer.

Thus, while the richest countries in the world are continuing to prosper, and the poorest countries (particularly in Africa) are becoming absolutely poorer, the rapidly industrializing Asian economies mentioned above are growing at rates rapid enough to produce an overall trend toward greater equalization of income around the world. Thus, cross-national studies such as the Human Development Report, which take nations rather than individuals as their units of analysis and do not weight countries by population size or adjust national currencies for purchasing power, often continue to show growing between-nation inequalities (Firebaugh 2003:123–40; Postrel 2002), whereas studies that make these weightings and adjustments (e.g., Bhalla 2002; Firebaugh 2003; Sala-i-Martin 2002) tend to report declines in Gini coefficients and similar indices of inequality in recent years.

The mischief comes when popular media pick up such research findings and broadcast them in headlines flatly announcing declining inequalities. The public is likely to misinterpret such headlines as meaning that the poorest must be doing better, and therefore, that there is no longer much need for concern about inequalities in the world. This is not to deny the value of Gini coefficients and other such measures as analytical tools. But as Firebaugh (2003:73) acknowledges, there may be merit in developing an "alternative conceptualization of *gap inequality*" that "combines the notion of widening gaps with the [economist's] conventional notion of inequality" (Firebaugh's emphasis).

Firebaugh's (2003) argument that inequality between nations appears to be declining, largely as a result of Asian industrialization, seems sharply at odds with the predictions of Myrdal and the dependency theorists, who have expected inequalities among nations to grow as a consequence of global capitalist market forces (see Firebaugh 2003:170–73, 201–03). Yet there may be a way to reconcile these two seemingly contradictory perspectives. As noted earlier, the two perspectives rest on two different conceptions of inequality. Firebaugh, using Gini coefficients and similar indices, focuses largely on what is happening in the middle portions of the world income distribution, especially regarding the upward movement of the large Asian economies, while dependency theorists are more concerned with what is happening at the extremes of wealth and poverty, and with the widening gulf that separates the richest from the poorest.

Firebaugh readily acknowledges widening gaps, but these are not his main concern. He views them largely as mathematical artifacts of any growth process (2003:72–73). Firebaugh's views are generally in keeping with neoclassical economic convergence theory (2003:171–73), which predicts that increasing global trade will tend to result in greater income growth in market-integrated developing nations and greater economic equality among nations. This view denies that the advantages of the rich are won at the expense of the poor. Nations in sub-Saharan Africa, to them, are not poor and getting poorer due to capitalist exploitation; on the contrary, they would be doing better if they were more fully integrated into the global economy. Convergence theorists disagree among themselves regarding the prospects for income growth in the rich countries. Some believe that such prospects are limited by the law of diminishing returns (Solow 1956), while others are optimistic that new research and development will continue to open new horizons for future growth, as revolutions in information technology have previously done (Firebaugh 2003:171–73). The latter school sees an economic world with a floor of absolute poverty, but no ceiling. Instead of the natural limits to growth seen by many demographers and ecologists (e.g., Meadows, Meadows, Randers, and Behrens 1972), these economic and technological optimists see only endless sky.

Critics of globalization, on the other hand, are not persuaded that global trade will lift all boats. They point to the crisis of foreign debt in poor nations that governments and banks in the rich nations are only recently addressing squarely. The report of a poverty summit conference organized by the Latin American Parliament (Olson 2001) observed that at birth, each child in Latin America already owed the equivalent of $1,550 in foreign debt—a sum that often exceeded a family's annual income. By 2001, governments had amassed a combined

$750 billion in foreign debt, or 36 percent of the region's annual GDP, consolidating U.S. economic dominance over Latin America. Trapped in a vicious cycle of debt, debtor nations continued to make interest payments on loans for which they were unable to pay off the principal. Hence, they did not have the resources to make public investments in health, education, and economic development that would help to enable them to rise out of poverty.

Compounding the problem of international debt is the problem of capital flight. This is particularly a problem when upper classes in developing countries invest their wealth in the more stable economies of the developed world, thus draining needed resources from their own economies. Economic inequalities within Latin American countries, such as Brazil and Mexico, remain among the highest in the world as measured by Gini coefficients and Lorenz curves. While the upper classes in these countries live in luxury, 50 of every 1,000 Latin American children die before their sixth birthday (Olson 2001). In Latin America and Africa particularly, the burden of foreign debt lies like a lead weight on hopes for the future.

Whether economic inequality among nations is increasing in recent years seems to depend largely on how we define and measure inequality, but there is no doubt that the absolute gap between the richest and the poorest nations continues to widen rapidly. There is evidence, meanwhile, that economic inequalities within most nations, including China, India, the former Soviet Union, and the United States, as measured by Gini coefficients and similar indices (Firebaugh 2003:152–66), are increasing as Myrdal would have predicted.[7] When we look within rather than among nations, we observe widening gaps between rich and poor, as with the gap between rural areas and urban centers of growth in China (Peng 1999). Although some argue that widening inequalities are not a matter of great concern so long as economic growth benefits the poor as well as the rich (Postrel 2002), the absolute gains of the rich vastly exceed those of the poor. Meanwhile, the poorest of the poor, primarily in Africa, grow not just relatively but absolutely poorer, and the gulf that separates them from the rest of humanity grows ever wider.

NOTES

1. WHAT IS THE MATTHEW EFFECT?

1. The text of Matthew (13:12) comes from the King James translation of the Bible, which Merton praised for its stately language. The New Revised Standard Version (NRSV) of the same verse reads as follows: "For to those who have, more will be given, and they will have an abundance; but from those who have nothing, even what they have will be taken away."

2. Stratification theorists associated with the former camp include Mc-Clelland (1961), who attributes differences in economic development among nations largely to levels of achievement motivation in their populations, and Davis and Moore (1945), who trace inequalities to the scarcity of talented personnel available to fill a society's most functionally important positions. Theorists in the latter camp include most conflict theorists from Marx onward, who generally attribute inequalities to the subjugation and exploitation of subordinate groups by dominant groups or classes. Insofar as conflict theorists recognize that dominant groups use their resources to command still more resources, they implicitly acknowledge the operation of Matthew effects. Turner (1984:73) notes that Lenski's (1966) theory of stratification, which synthesizes elements of conflict and evolutionary theory, clearly recognizes that when dominant groups consolidate power, they use that power to gain and consolidate still more power. Similarly, Marxist theories of stratification stress that investing capital to accumulate still more capital is a systemic feature of capitalism. Power and wealth are thus seen to create self-amplifying feedback loops.

3. As the name implies, the concept of the Matthew effect is an ancient one. Merton initially attributed the idea to the author of the biblical gospel according to Matthew, where it actually appears twice (first in 13:12 and again in 25:29). Merton later noted that variations of the saying appear also in Mark 4:25 and still again in Luke 8:18 and 19:26 (Merton 1988:609n). He credits theologian Marinus de Jonge for tracing the idea even further into the past. De Jonge notes that "it is highly likely that [Jesus] took over a general saying, current in the Jewish (and/or Hellenistic) Wisdom circles—see, e.g., Proverbs 9:9, Daniel 2:21, or Martialis, Epigr. V 81: 'Semper pauper eris, si pauper es, Aemiliane. Dantur opes nullis [nunc] nisi divitibus' ["You will always be poor if you are poor, Aemilianus. Wealth is given nowadays to none but the rich."] (Merton 1988:609n). Merton introduced the notion of Matthew effects, though not yet by that name, into the social sciences as early as 1942, when he remarked on the "accumulation of differential advantages for certain segments of the population, differentials that are not bound up with demonstrated differences in capacity (1973 [1942]:273).

4. The saying appears in two very different metaphorical contexts. In Matthew 13, Mark 4, and Luke 8, it accompanies the parable of the sower whose seed, when it falls on fertile ground, yields a rich harvest. In Matthew 25 and Luke 19, it appears in the context of the parable of the talents, urging the greatest possible development of what we are entrusted with. Though the latter parable is economic on a literal level, those who invoke it to justify extreme economic inequalities will be hard-pressed to reconcile their interpretation with Jesus's numerous other teachings on wealth and poverty (Wallis 2005).

5. Public awareness of the importance of feedback loops in nature and society is likely to grow in coming years as we begin to recognize their role in creating runaway change. Knowledge of feedback loops is essential to understanding the dynamics of climate change (Homer-Dixon 2007).

6. Merton (1968b:105) defines functions as "those observed consequences which make for the adaptation or adjustment of a given system." I have amended this usage slightly, replacing "adaptation and adjustment" with "sustainability," on the grounds that the latter term suggests connections and applications of functionalism to a host of vital contemporary issues, such as energy, environment, and war, without (I hope) unduly distorting Merton's original concept.

7. Downward spirals of disadvantage operate in a similar manner, except that diminishing advantages are deamplifed rather than amplified.

2. MATTHEW EFFECTS IN SCIENCE AND TECHNOLOGY

1. The concept of the Matthew effect was only one among many of Merton's enduring contributions to social theory. To gain a sense of the breadth and scope of his intellectual legacy, see Clark, Modgil, and Modgil (1990) and Crothers (1987). Other scholars had similar notions during this period, including economist Gunnar Myrdal (discussed in Chapter 3), who developed the concept of circular causation, and science historian Derek J. de Solla Price (1965:511), who conjectured that "the more a paper is cited the more likely it is to be cited thereafter."

2. Merton attributes the persistence of Matthew effects in part to their positive consequences for science as a whole. Goldstone (1979) challenges this functionalist analysis, arguing that such effects can be adequately explained in terms of individual behavior without recourse to functionalist explanations. Dannefer (2003) has observed that Merton himself was ambivalent about the functionality of Matthew effects in science. As a functionalist, he recognized that such effects highlight the work of exceptional scientists and thereby promote the efficiency of scientific communication systems. Yet he also readily acknowledged the dysfunctions they create when they unfairly overlook the contributions of lesser-known scientists, resulting in resentment and the unintended suppression of talent.

3. Cole and Cole's methodology may understate the strength of Matthew effects in science. The authors' method is to compare the quality of papers by high-ranking and low-ranking scientists as measured by the number of times they are cited. However, as the authors themselves acknowledge (1973:199), some papers by lesser scientists may be overlooked or undervalued. To the extent that this occurs, the Coles' method would underestimate the quality of the work of less eminent relative to more eminent scientists. Thus the Coles' method of measuring quality to gauge the strength of Matthew effects may, ironically, be distorted by the Matthew effect itself.

4. Consider the dispute over whether Dorothy Swaine Thomas received due credit for the Thomas theorem, often attributed solely to her future husband, W.I. Thomas, as discussed in Merton (1995b) and Smith (1999). Merton (1995b:395) observes that Dorothy Swaine Thomas, as

the less renowned coauthor, may have been the inadvertent victim of a Matthew effect compounded by gender bias.

5. In chemistry, *autocatalysis* refers to the process whereby an initial chemical reaction produces catalysts needed to sustain further reactions.

3. MATTHEW EFFECTS IN THE ECONOMY

1. While capitalist economies in particular are fueled largely by the drive to accumulate private material wealth, Merton argued that science is driven more by the pursuit of symbolic than material rewards (1968a; 1988:219–23). Scientists are motivated largely by a desire for "cognitive . . . and reputational wealth"—not only the intrinsic desire for knowledge, but also the extrinsic desire for the recognition of one's peers. This recognition is not achieved by hoarding one's product (scientific knowledge) for oneself, but rather by giving it away freely to the scientific community. Merton contended that the economy of knowledge is not an economy of scarcity, "for a fund of knowledge is not diminished through exceedingly intensive use . . . indeed, it is presumably augmented" (1988:620). In the gift economy of science, the more one gives away, the more one receives, and the resource of scientific knowledge is continually replenished and expanded in the process. It is conceivable that the postindustrial information economies of the future will come increasingly to resemble this idealized gift economy of science, though it is perhaps more likely that science itself will be run increasingly along business lines, with private profitability as its ultimate aim.

2. A million dollars is not what it used to be. The title of energy baron T. Boone Pickens' (2008) autobiography is *The First Billion is the Hardest.*

3. Despite striking convergences between Merton's Matthew effect and Myrdal's circular causation, there are also important differences. Merton, much influenced by the structural-functional theory of his mentor, Talcott Parsons (1951), was inclined to ascribe to social systems a natural tendency toward stable equilibrium, though he freely acknowledged the existence of disequilibrating dysfunctions (Merton 1968b). Myrdal, by contrast, was considerably more skeptical of the existence of natural equilibria of any kind (1957:9ff), doubting even the neoclassical economic orthodoxy that prices are determined through an

equilibrium of supply and demand. Stable states occur, he acknowledged, but they do so by accident when relevant forces happen to be in equipoise. As one force gains strength or another weakens, the system inevitably is set back into motion again and has no "desire" to return to its previous state, or even to another stable state. Dynamism and instability, not order and stability, are the natural order of things in economic and other social systems. Another difference is that Merton's Matthew effects increase inequalities by definition, while Myrdal's circular causation, though usually increasing inequalities, may also diminish them in some circumstances, as in the example previously given of the mitigation of race relations through the mutual interaction of white tolerance and the advancement of black living standards (1944:76). This would exemplify a virtuous circle, though Myrdal does not seem to use the term.

4. Circular causation is at the heart of popular theories touting the benefits of positive thinking. In a sophisticated version of the popular creed, Kanter (2004) examines the psychology and sociology of winning and losing streaks in sports and business. She argues that confidence enhances performance and that enhanced performance leads to victory, creating a "cycle of success." In sports, social supports, such as an enthusiastic fan base and positive media attention, further contribute to success. The dynamics of losing are the dynamics of winning in reverse, creating "doom loops" and "death spirals." "The system has momentum," Kanter contends, creating both crests of victory and undertows of defeat (2004:94–95). For Kanter, athletic competition is a metaphor for corporate competition, where similar cycles of success and failure are commonly observed.

5. For a more detailed discussion of the measurement of inequality, and the general direction of national and world trends in the distribution of resources, see the Appendix's trends in economic inequality.

4. MATTHEW EFFECTS IN POLITICS AND PUBLIC POLICY

1. Economic advantage may be analytically distinct from political and status advantage, but these factors tend to be empirically linked and mutually reinforcing. Max Weber's (1946 [1922]) essay on class, status, and party is the classic frame for this discussion.

5. MATTHEW EFFECTS IN EDUCATION AND CULTURE

1. Howley (2001) appears in an electronic journal (see references); the quotation appears in the acknowledgments at the top of the article.

2. Different authors use the term *social capital* in somewhat different ways (see, e.g., Coleman 1990; Fukuyama 1995; Putnam 2000). In Bourdieu's usage, the term refers essentially to the networks and support systems upon which social actors rely to maintain and improve their social positions. The mathematics of networks seems to predispose these to produce Matthew effects: The larger a network's size—measured by its number of nodes and links—the more nodes are available to link to future nodes. Thus, other things equal, larger networks can add nodes more rapidly than smaller networks. By analogy, if a small and a large snowball are rolling down the same hill at the same speed, the large snowball accumulates more snow in the same interval of time.

6. IMPLICATIONS AND CONCLUSIONS

1. We find the term *Matthew effect* invoked, metaphorically if not literally, even in the distant field of astronomy. Jones (2007:66) explains that planets form when dust grains collide and coagulate to form planetesimals, or little planets. Smaller planetesimals are drawn by gravitational force to larger planetesimals, which eventually forms new planets as the large become larger. Jones describes this as a Matthew effect.

2. Public policy in a democracy, at least in theory, reflects our core values. Elsewhere we have argued that American ideology is severely conflicted at the level of core values, and that we have not one, but three competing national ideologies (Rigney 2001:94–100). First, traditional conservatism, with its roots in antiquity, upholds above all the values of social order, hierarchical authority, and tradition. Religious and military conservatives, with their emphases on law and order, patriarchy, and patriotism, are representative of this value system. Second, libertarianism—also known as classical or nineteenth-century liberalism, not to be confused with contemporary liberalism—is a strong strand in American ideological discourse, upholding the more modern values of individual liberty and individual responsibility. Libertarianism is associated historically with the rise of capitalism, and entails a defense of free markets relatively unhindered by governmen-

tal interference. Finally, social democracy—or contemporary liberalism—is the third primary color in the American ideological palette.
Its core value is the achievement of greater political and economic
equality in society. Its roots lie in organized labor movements; in liberal religious movements, such as those that have advocated the aboli-
tion of slavery and the expansion of civil rights; and in democratic
political movements seeking to empower the less powerful. While social democrats do not seek absolute equality, which is unattainable in
any event, they believe that the extreme degrees of inequality that we
observe in the United States and the world are morally intolerable.

3. Some forms of intergenerational transfer redistribute resources not
   from older to younger generations, as inheritance typically does, but
   rather from younger to older. Social Security and Medicare payments
   to retirees in the enormous baby boom generation will represent a
   massive transfer of resources running opposite the usual direction of
   inheritance (Chisolm 2006).

4. Samuelson (2002a) contends that the economic recovery of 2002 was
   sustained in considerable part by trickle-up consumption on the part
   of moderate-income households.

APPENDIX: TRENDS IN ECONOMIC INEQUALITY

1. Sen (1997 [1973]: 24–46) offers a systematic overview of the relative
   merits of alternative methods of measuring inequality, including the
   Gini and Theil measures. For further discussions of the measurement
   of inequality, see Wolff 1995/2002:75–88; Ryscavage 1999:24–44; and
   Firebaugh 2003:70–84.

2. Keister's (2005) analysis seems to challenge the view that the United
   States is becoming increasingly caste-like. She notes that, contrary to
   our national mythology, rates of mobility in the distribution of wealth
   in the United States were relatively low prior to 1900 (2005:245), and
   that the late twentieth century spawned a range of new opportunities
   for the acquisition of wealth, particularly in advanced technology.

3. Cauchon's (2007) analysis of Federal Reserve data leads him to conclude that the "growing divide between the rich and poor in America
   is more generation gap than class conflict. . . . Overwhelmingly, the
   rich are older folks." He notes that "nearly all additional wealth created
   in the USA since 1989 has gone to people 55 and older." This conclu-

sion is potentially misleading, however. Cauchon's analysis glaringly omits to mention that while older Americans as a whole have never been more prosperous, this general prosperity masks widening economic inequalities within the fifty-and-over population since 1980 (Dannefer 1987; Gist, Figueiredo, and Ng-Baumhackl. 2001). A relatively small number of wealthy and super-wealthy elders can drive up the average wealth of the age group as a whole, creating the illusion of broadly distributed wealth and concealing extreme class differences among the elderly themselves. When a billionaire walks into a room full of thousandaires, mathematically, the average person in the room suddenly becomes a multimillionaire.

4. For a critical view of dependency theory, see Velasco (2002).

5. A useful resource for educating oneself on the issue of global inequalities is the University of California Atlas of Global Inequality (2008). Here we find references and links to research studies on several different sides of the debate, giving a more rounded picture than one is likely to find in ideological sources that represent only staunch pro-globalization or antiglobalization perspectives.

6. Some are skeptical of the quality and validity of these data. See Aslund (2001), Firebaugh (2003:186–87), and Postrel (2002).

7. Firebaugh observes that in agrarian times, prior to the industrial revolution, inequalities within societies around the world were far more pronounced than inequalities among societies. Firebaugh terms this pattern the "inequality transition." In phase one of the transition, from the early nineteenth to the mid-twentieth century, inequalities among nations increased as the industrializing Western nations pulled away from the rest of the world. By the late twentieth century, developing nations, particularly in Asia, entered a period of intense industrialization, ushering in phase two of the inequality transition. In phase two, industrializing nations, such as India and China, have begun to catch up to developed Western economies, reducing between-nation inequalities. But what about within-nation inequalities? In phase one, these tended to widen due to the gap between lower-paid agricultural labor and higher-paid industrial labor (Kuznets 1955; Firebaugh 2003:30, 93–95). In phase two, developed nations have experienced growing internal inequalities as well, but for a different reason. These nations have shrinking industrial sectors but growing service sectors. Because the service sector is extremely diverse, subsuming occupa-

tions as diverse as banker and burger flipper, occupational inequalities in the service sector lead to growing inequalities within the economies of the richest countries. Firebaugh (2003:196–201) acknowledges that no single factor explains these trends. Factors contributing to the current pattern of diminishing between-nation inequality (as measured by Gini coefficients) and growing within-nation inequality include the growth of the industrial sector in developing countries and of the service sector in developed countries, the convergence of progrowth governmental policies (e.g., in trade and education) around the world, and the emergence of space-independent information technology, helping to integrate developing countries into the world economy. With the decline of communism and the promise of a demographic windfall as poor countries bring their population problems under control, Firebaugh is generally optimistic that the globalization of the world economy will benefit most of the world's people.

REFERENCES

Allison, Paul D., J. Scott Long, and Tad Krauze. 1982. "Cumulative Advantage and Inequality in Science." *American Sociological Review* 47 (October): 615–625.

Allison, Paul D. and John A. Stewart. 1974. "Productivity Differences among Scientists: Evidence for Accumulative Advantage." *American Sociological Review* 39 (August): 596–606.

Alonso, William and Paul Starr, eds. 1987. *The Politics of Numbers.* New York: Russell Sage.

American Federation of Labor and Congress of Industrial Organizations (AFL-CIO). 2008. *2008 Executive PayWatch.* Available online at http://www.aflcio.org/corporatewatch/paywatch/ (accessed July 12, 2008).

Andre, Claire and Manuel Velasquez. 1990. "The Just World Theory." *Issues in Ethics* 3 (2). Available online at http://www.scu.edu/ethics/publications/iie/v3n2/justworld.html (accessed July 31, 2008).

Aristotle. 1987 [~340 BCE]. *Politics.* In *A New Aristotle Reader,* ed. J.L. Ackrill, 507–556. Princeton, NJ: Princeton University Press.

Arthur, W. Brian. 1990. "Positive Feedback in the Economy." *Scientific American* 262 (2): 92–99.

——. 1994. *Increasing Returns and Path Dependence in the Economy.* Ann Arbor: University of Michigan Press.

——. 1996. "Increasing Returns and the New World of Business." *Harvard Business Review* 74 (July/August): 101–109.

Aslund, Anders. 2001. *Building Capitalism: The Transformation of the Former Soviet Bloc.* Cambridge: Cambridge University Press.

Autor, David, Lawrence F. Katz, and Melissa S. Kearney. 2008. "Trends in U.S. Wage Inequality: Revising the Revisionists." *Review of Economics and Statistics* 90 (May): 300–323.

Awaida, May and John R. Beech. 1995. "Children's Lexical and Sublexical Development while Learning to Read." *Journal of Experimental Education* 63 (2): 97–113.

Bahr, Peter R. 2007. "Double Jeopardy: Testing the Effects of Multiple Basic Skill Deficiencies on Successful Remediation." *Research in Higher Education* 48 (6): 695–725.

Bai, Matt. 2007. "The Poverty Platform." *New York Times Magazine,* June 10, 66ff.

Banerjee, Abhijit V. and Sendhil Mullainathan. 2008. "Limited Attention and Income Distribution." *American Economic Review* (May): 489–493.

Bartlett, Donald L. and James B. Steele. 2000. *The Great American Tax Dodge.* Boston: Little Brown.

Bast, Janwillem and Pieter Reitsma. 1997. "Matthew Effects in Reading." *Multivariate Behavioral Research* 32: 135–167.

——. 1998. "Analyzing the Development of Individual Differences in Terms of Matthew Effects in Reading." *Developmental Psychology* 34 (6): 1373–1399.

Beeghley, Leonard. 1989. *The Structure of Social Stratification.* Boston: Allyn and Bacon.

Berninger, Virginia W. 1999. "Overcoming the Matthew Effect." *Issues in Education* 5 (1): 45–54.

Bhalla, Surjit S. 2002. *Imagine There's No Country.* Washington, DC: Institute for International Economics.

Bishai, David and Andrew Poon. 2001. *Does the Law of Diminishing Returns Apply to Infant Mortality Decline?* Baltimore, MD: Johns Hopkins University School of Public Health.

Blashfield, R.K., S.B. Guze, J.S. Strauss, M.M. Katz, and R.E. Kendell. 1982. "Invisible Colleges and the Matthew Effect" (comments). *Schizophrenia Bulletin* 8 (1): 1–6.

Bluestone, Barry, and Bennett Harrison. 1982. *The Deindustrialization of America.* New York: Basic Books.

Bonitz, Manfred. 1997. "The Scientific Talents of Nations." *Libri* 47 (4): 206–213.

——. 2002. "Ranking of Nations and Heightened Competition in Matthew Zone Journals: Two Faces of the Matthew Effect for Countries." *Library Trends* 50 (Winter): 440–460.

——. 2005. "The Matthew Effect for Countries: Its Impact on Information Science." *ISSI Newsletter* 1 (3): 7–10. Available online at http://www.issi-society.info/archives/newsletter03print.pdf (accessed July 31, 2008).

Boshara, Ray. 2003. "The $6,000 Solution." *Atlantic Monthly,* January/February, 91–95.

Bourdieu, Pierre. 1984. *Distinction*. Cambridge, MA: Harvard University Press.

——. 1986. "The Forms of Capital." In *Handbook for Theory and Research for the Sociology of Education,* ed. J.G. Richardson, 241–258. New York: Greenwood.

Bowen, William G., Martin A Kurzweil, and Eugene M. Tobin. 2005. *Equity and Excellence in American Higher Education*. Charlottesville: University of Virginia Press.

Boyer, Ernest L. 1990. *Scholarship Reconsidered: Priorities of the Professoriate.* Princeton, NJ: Carnegie Foundation for the Advancement of Teaching.

Braun, Denny. 1997. *The Rich Get Richer: The Rise of Income Inequality in the United States and the World,* 2nd edition. Chicago: Nelson-Hall Publishers.

Broughton, Walter and Edgar W. Mills, Jr. 1980. "Resource Inequality and Accumulative Advantage: Stratification in the Ministry." *Social Forces* 58 (4): 1289–1301.

Buckley, Walter. 1967. *Sociology and Modern Systems Theory*. Englewood Cliffs, NJ: Prentice Hall.

Burstall, Clare. 1978. "The Matthew Effect in the Classroom." *Educational Research* 21 (1): 19–25.

Butcher, Kristin and David Card. 1991. "Immigration and Wages: Evidence from the 1980s." *American Economic Review* 90 (May): 292–296.

Caner, Asena and Edward Wolff. 2004. *Asset Poverty in the United States*. Annandale on Hudson, NY: Levy Economics Institute of Bard College. Available online at http://www.levy.org/pubs/ppb/ppb76.pdf (accessed July 31, 2008).

Cardozo, Fernando Henrique and Enzo Faletto. 1979. *Dependency and Development in Latin America*. Berkeley: University of California Press.

Casey, Rick. 2005. "Lottery Another Soak-the-Poor Endeavor." *San Antonio Express-News,* February 5, 13B.

CASL (Center on Accelerating Student Learning). 2001. "Background." Vanderbilt University, Nashville, TN. Available online at http://kc.vanderbilt.edu/casl/background.html (accessed July 31, 2008).

Cassady, John. 1995. "Who Killed the Middle Class?" *New Yorker,* October 6, 113ff.

Cauchon, Dennis. 2007. "Generation Gap? About $200,000." *USA Today,* May 20), 1ff.

Center for Responsive Politics. 2005. "The Big Picture." Available online at http://www.opensecrets.org (accessed July 12, 2005).

Cervantes, Mario and Dominique Guellec. 2002. "The Brain Drain: Old Myths, New Realities." *OECD Observer* 230 (January). Available online at http://www.oecdobserver.org/news/fullstory.php/aid/673/The_brain_drain: old myths, new realities.html (accessed August 1, 2008).

Chisolm, Patrick. 2006. "Triumph of the Redistributionist Left." *Christian Science Monitor,* January 23, 25.

Clark, Jon, Celia Modgil, and Sohan Modgil, eds. 1990. *Robert K. Merton: Consensus and Controversy.* London: Falmer Press.

Clark, Shirley and Mary Corcoran. 1986. "Perspectives on the Professional Socialization of Women Faculty: A Case of Accumulative Disadvantage?" *Journal of Higher Education* 57 (1): 20–43.

Cloward, Richard A. and Lloyd B. Ohlin. 1960. *Delinquency and Opportunity.* 1960. New York: Free Press.

Cole, Jonathan. 1979. *Fair Science: Women in the Scientific Community.* New York: Free Press.

Cole, Jonathan R. and Stephen Cole. 1973. *Social Stratification in Science.* Chicago: University of Chicago Press.

Cole, Stephen. 1970. "Professional Standing and the Reception of Scientific Discoveries." *American Journal of Sociology* 76 (2): 286–306. Reprinted in Jonathan R. and Steven Cole, *Social Stratification in Science* (Chicago: University of Chicago Press, 191–215).

Cole, Jonathan and Burton Singer. 1991. "A Theory of Limited Differences: Explaining the Productivity Puzzle in Science." In *The Outer Circle: Women in the Scientific Comnmunity*, ed. H. Zuckerman, J.R. Cole, and J.T. Bruer, 277–310. New York: Norton.

Coleman, James S. 1990. *Foundations of Social Theory.* Cambridge, MA: Belknap/Harvard University Press.

Collins, Chuck, Betsy Leonard-Wright, and Holly Sklar. 1999. *Shifting Fortunes: The Perils of the Growing American Wealth Gap.* Boston: United for a Fair Economy.

Cox, Harvey. 1999. "The Market as God." *Atlantic Monthly,* March, 18–23.

Cox, W. Michael and Richard Alm. 1999. *Myths of Rich and Poor.* New York: Basic Books.

Crane, Diana. 1965. "Scientists at Major and Minor Universities." *American Sociological Review* 30 (October): 699–714.

——. 1972. *Invisible Colleges.* Chicago: University of Chicago Press.

Crespi, Barnard J. 2004. "Vicious Circles: Positive Feedback in Major Evolutionary and Ecological Transitions." *Trends in Ecology and Evolution* 19 (12): 627–633.

Crothers, Charles. 1987. *Robert K. Merton.* Chichester, W. Sussex: Ellis Horwood.

Cunningham, Anne and Keith Stanovich. 1998. "What Reading Does for the Mind." *American Educator* 22 (1): 8–15.

Dannefer, Dale. 1987. "Aging as Intracohort Differentiation: Accentuation, the Matthew Effect, and the Life Course." *Sociological Forum* 2 (2): 211–236.

——. 2003. "Cumulative Advantage/Disadvantage and the Life Course: Cross-Fertilizing Age and Social Science Theory." *Journals of Gerontology Series B: Psychological Sciences and Social Sciences* 58 (6): S327–S337.

Dannefer, Dale and Lynn Gannon. 2005. "The Matthew Effect and Social Processes: Cumulative Advantage/Disadvantage as a 'Law of the Life Course.'" Paper presented at the annual meeting of the American Sociological Association, Philadelphia, August 12.

Davis, Kingsley and Wilbert E. Moore. 1945. "Some Principles of Stratification." *American Sociological Review* 10 (2): 242–249.

Delbanco, Andrew. 2007. "Scandals of Higher Education." *New York Review of Books* 54 (5): 42–46.

Deleeck, Herman, Karel Van den Bosch, and Lieve de Lathouwer, ed. 1992. *Poverty and the Adequacy of Social Security in the EC: A Comparative Analysis.* Brookfield, VT: Avebury.

de Solla Price, Derek J. 1965. "Networks of Scientific Papers." *Science* 149 (3683): 510–515.

Diamond, Jared. 1997. *Guns, Germs, and Steel: The Fates of Human Societies.* New York: Norton.

DiPrete, Thomas A. and Gregory M. Eirich. 2006. "Cumulative Advantage as a Mechanism for Inequality: A Review of Theoretical and Empirical Developments." *Annual Review of Sociology* 32 (1): 271–297.

Douthat, Ross and Reihan Salam. 2005. "The Party of Sam's Club." *Weekly Standard,* November 14, 11.

Durkheim, Emile. 1958 [1895]. *The Rules of Sociological Method.* New York: Free Press.

Dzakpasu, Susie, K.S. Joseph, Michael S. Kramer, and Alexander C. Allen. 2000. "The Matthew Effect: Infant Mortality in Canada and Internationally." *Pediatrics* 106 (1): e5. Available online at http://www.pediatrics.org/cgi/content/full/106/1/e5 (accessed August 1, 2008).

Economist. 2003. "Pigs, Pay and Power." June 28, 7–9.

Ehrenreich, Barbara. 2001. *Nickeled and Dimed: On (Not) Getting By in America*. New York: Metropolitan Books.

Elster, Jon. 1982. "Marxism, Functionalism, and Game Theory: The Case for Methodological Individualism." *Theory and Society* 11 (4): 453–482.

——. 1990. "Merton's Functionalism and the Unintended Consequences of Action." In *Robert K. Merton: Consensus and Controversy*, ed. Jon Clark, Celia Modgil, and Sohan Modgil, 129–135. London and New York: Falmer Press.

Feagin, Joe. 2006. *Systemic Racism: A Theory of Oppression*. New York: Routledge.

Firebaugh, Glenn. 2003. *The New Geography of Global Income Inequality*. Cambridge, MA: Harvard University Press.

Fogg, Piper. 2005. "Harvard President Wonders Aloud about Women in Science and Math." *Chronicle of Higher Education*, January 28, A12.

Fox, Mary Frank. 1981. "Sex, Salary, and Achievement: Reward-Dualism in Academia." *Sociology of Education* 54 (2): 71–84.

——. 1985. "Publication, Performance, and Reward in Science and Scholarship." In *Higher Education: Handbook of Theory and Research*, ed. J. Smart, 255–282. New York: Agathan.

Frank, André Gunder. 1993. *The World System*. London: Routledge.

Frank, Robert H. and Philip J. Cook. 1996. *The Winner-Take-All Society*. New York: Penguin.

Frank, Thomas. 2005. *What's the Matter With Kansas?* New York: Henry Holt.

Freiberger, Paul and Michael Swaine. 2000. *Fire in the Valley: The Making of the Personal Computer*, 2nd edition. New York: McGraw-Hill.

Friedman, Thomas. 2000. *The Lexus and the Olive Tree*. New York: Anchor.

——. 2005. *The World Is Flat*. New York: Farrar, Straus and Giroux.

Fukuyama, Francis. 1995. *Trust: Social Virtues and the Creation of Prosperity*. New York: Free Press.

Gabris, Gerald T. and Kenneth Mitchell. 1988. "The Impact of Merit Raise Scores on Employee Attitudes: The Matthew Effect of Performance Appraisal." *Public Personnel Management* 17 (4): 369–386.

Garfunkel, Joseph M., Martin H. Ulshen, Harvey J. Hamrick, and Edward E. Lawson. 1994. "Effect of Institutional Prestige on Reviewers' Recommendations and Editorial Decisions." *Journal of the American Medical Association* 272 (2): 137–138.

Gates, William H. Sr. and Chuck Collins. 2002. *Wealth and Our Commonwealth: Why America Should Tax Accumulated Fortunes*. Boston: Beacon.

Gist, John, Carlos Figueiredo, and Mitja Ng-Baumhackl. 2001. "Beyond 50: A Report to the Nation on Economic Security." AARP Public Policy Institute. Available online at http://www.aarp.org/beyond50 (accessed July 31, 2008).

Gladwell, Malcolm. 2000. *The Tipping Point*. Boston: Little, Brown.

———. 2008. *Outliers: The Story of Success*. New York: Little, Brown.

Gleick, James. 1987. *Chaos: Making a New Science*. New York: Penguin.

Goffman, Erving. 1963. *Stigma*. Englewood Cliffs, NJ: Prentice-Hall.

Goldin, Claudia and Lawrence Katz. 2008. *The Race between Education and Technology*. Cambridge, MA: Harvard University Press.

Goldstone, J.A. 1979. "A Deductive Explanation of the Matthew Effect in Science." *Social Studies of Science* 9 (8): 385–391.

Goodstein, David and James Woodward. 1999. "Inside Science." *American Scholar* 68 (4): 83–90.

Graef, Crystal. 1991. *In Search of Excess: The Overcompensation of American Executives*. New York: Norton.

Graetz, Michael J. and Ian Shapiro. 2005. *Death by a Thousand Cuts: The Fight over Taxing Inherited Wealth*. Princeton, NJ: Princeton University Press.

Hanish, Christine, John J. Horan, Beth Keen, Carolyn Cox St. Peter, Sherry Dyche Ceperich, and Julie F. Beasley. 1995: "The Scientific Stature of Counseling Psychology Training Programs." *Counseling Psychology* 23 (1): 82–101.

Hall, Robert and Alvin Rabushka. 1995. *The Flat Tax*, 2nd edition. Stanford, CA: Hoover Institution Press.

Hearn, James. C. 1991. "Academic and Nonacademic Influences on the College Destinations of 1980 High School Graduates." *Sociology of Education* 64 (July): 158–171.

Hedström, Peter and Richard Swedberg, eds. 1998. *Social Mechanisms: An Analytical Approach to Social Theory*. Cambridge: Cambridge University Press.

Hernandez, Donald J. and Suzanne Macartney. 2008. "Racial-Ethnic Inequality in Child Well-Being from 1985–2004." FCD Policy Brief #9. New York: Foundation for Child Development.

Hofstadter, Richard. 1992. *Social Darwinism in American Thought*. Boston: Beacon.

Homer-Dixon, Thomas. 2007. "A Swiftly Melting Planet." *New York Times*, October 4, A29.

Howley, Craig. 2001. "The Matthew Principle: A West Virginia Replication?"

Education Policy Analysis Archives 3 (18). Available online at http://epaa. asu.edu/epaa/v3n18.html (accessed July 31, 2008).

Huber, Joan C. 1998. "Cumulative Advantage and Success-Breeds-Success: The Value of Time Pattern Analysis." *Journal of the American Society for Information Science* 49 (5): 471–476.

Hunt, James G. and John D. Blair. 1987. "Content, Process, and the Matthew Effect among Management Academics." *Journal of Management* 13 (2): 191–210.

Hulse, Carl and David M. Herszenhorn. 2008. "G.O.P. Exodus in House Bodes Ill for Fall Success." *New York Times,* January 31, A16.

Ishaq, Ashfaq. 2001. "On the Global Digital Divide." *Finance and Development: A Quarterly Magazine of the IMF* 36 (3). Available online at http:// www.imf.org/external/pubs/ft/fandd/2001/09/Ishaq.htm (accessed June 2, 2009).

Jencks, Christopher. 1987. "The Politics of Income Measurement." In *The Politics of Numbers,* ed. William Alonso and Paul Starr, 83–131. New York: Russell Sage.

Johnston, David Cay. 2001. "Dozens of Rich Americans Join in Fight to Retain the Estate Tax." *The New York Times,* February 14, A1.

——. 2003. *Perfectly Legal.* New York: Portfolio.

——. 2005. "Richest Are Leaving Even the Rich Far Behind." In *Class Matters,* 182–191. New York: Times Books/Henry Holt.

——. 2007. "Report Says That the Rich Are Getting Richer Faster, Much Faster." *New York Times,* December 15, C3.

Jones, Barrie W. 2007. *Discovering the Solar System.* Hoboken, NJ: Wiley and Sons.

Kanter, Rosabeth Moss. 1977. *Men and Women of the Corporation.* New York: Basic Books.

——. 2004. *Confidence: How Winning and Losing Streaks Begin and End.* New York: Crown.

Keister, Lisa A. 2000. *Wealth in America: Trends in Wealth Inequality.* Cambridge: Cambridge University Press.

——. 2005. *Getting Rich.* New York: Cambridge University Press.

Kennickell, Arthur B. 2009. "Ponds and Streams: Wealth and Income in the U.S., 1989 to 2007." Federal Reserve Board Finance and Economics Discussion Series. Available online at http://wwwfederalreserve.gov/pubs/ feds/2009/200913/ (accessed May 13, 2009).

Kerckhoff, Alan C. and Elizabeth Glennie. 1999. "The Matthew Effect in

American Education." *Research in Sociology of Education and Socialization* 12: 35–66.

Kinsley, Michael. 1995. "The Flat Tax Society." *New Yorker,* May 1, 8–9.

——. 2001. "Shining C: Land of Opportunity, Bush-Style." *Slate,* July 6. Available at www.slate.com (Accessed May 13, 2009).

Knapp, Peter. 1999. "Evolution, Complex Systems and the Dialectic." *Journal of World-Systems Research* 5 (1): 74–103. Available online at http://www.jwsr.ucr.edu/archive/vol5/number1/v5n1a4.php (Accessed September 11, 2009).

Koch, Wendy. 2008. "Minority Kids Make Healthy Gains." *USA Today,* January 28, 1.

Kochhar, Rakesh. 2004. *The Wealth of Hispanic Households: 1996 to 2002.* Washington, DC: Pew Hispanic Center. Available online at http://pewhispanic.org/files/reports/34.pdf (accessed August 1, 2008).

Kozol, Jonathan. 1991. *Savage Inequalities: Children in America's Schools.* New York: Crown.

Krugman, Paul. 2001. "An Injured City." *New York Times,* October 3, A23.

——. 2004. "The Death of Horatio Alger." *Nation,* January 5, 16–17.

Kuznets, Simon. 1955. "Economic Growth and Income Inequality." *American Economic Review* 45 (1): 1–28.

Landes, David. 1998. *The Wealth and Poverty of Nations.* New York: Norton.

Lenski, Gerhard. 1966. *Power and Privilege.* New York: McGraw-Hill.

Lenski, Gerhard and Jean Lenski. 1970. *Human Societies.* New York: McGraw-Hill.

Leonhardt, David. 2003. "Gap between Pay of Men and Women Smallest on Record." *New York Times,* February 17, 1ff.

Lerner, Melvin J. 1980. *The Belief in a Just World: A Fundamental Delusion.* New York: Plenum Press.

Levesque, Jeri. 2000. "Across the Great Divide." *Focus on Basics* 4 (C). Available online at http://www.gse.harvard.edu/~ncsall/fob/2000/levesque.html (accessed August 1, 2008).

Lievrouw, Leah A. 2000. "New Media: Networks vs. Bow Ties: Metaphors for the New Media Landscape." *International Communication Association Newsletter* 28 (3): 6–7.

Link, Bruce and Barry Milcarek. 1980. "Selection Factors in the Dispensation of Therapy: The Matthew Effect in the Allocation of Mental-Health Resources." *Journal of Health and Social Behavior* 21 (3): 279–290.

Long, J. Scott. 1990. "The Origins of Sex Differences in Science." *Social Forces*

68 (4): 1297–1315.

——. 1992. "Measures of Sex Differences in Scientific Productivity." *Social Forces* 71 (1): 159–178.

Lowenstein, Roger. 2007. "The Inequality Conundrum." *New York Times Magazine,* June 10, 11ff.

Mansson, Sven-Axel and Ulla-Carin Hedin 1999. "Breaking the Matthew Effect: On Women Leaving Prostitution." *International Journal of Social Welfare* 8 (1): 57–67.

Machiavelli, Niccolo. 1981 [1532]. *The Prince.* Trans. Daniel Donno. Toronto: Bantam.

Martell, Richard F., David M. Lane, and Cynthia Emrich. 1996. "Male-Female Differences: A Computer Simulation." *American Psychologist* 51 (2): 157–158.

Marwah, Sanjay and Mathieu Defleur. 2006. "Revisiting Merton: Continuities in the Theory of Anomie-and-Opportunity Structures." In *Sociological Theory and Criminological Research: Views from Europe and the United States,* ed. Mathiew Defleur, 57–76. Amsterdam: Elsevier/JAI Press.

Marx, Karl. 1967 [1867]. *Capital.* New York: International.

Marx, Karl and Frederick Engels. 1955 [1848]. *The Communist Manifesto.* Arlington Heights, IL: Harlan Davidson.

McCaffery, Edward J. 2002. *Fair Not Flat: How to Make the Tax System Better and Simpler.* Chicago: University of Chicago Press.

McClelland, David. 1961. *The Achieving Society.* Princeton, NJ: Van Nostrand.

McMahon, Martin J. Jr. and Clarence J. TeSelle. 2004. "The Matthew Effect and Federal Taxation." Paper presented at Boston College Law Review Symposium, February.

Meadows, Donella, Dennis Meadows, Jorgen Randers, and William W. Behrens, III. 1972. *The Limits to Growth.* New York: Universe Books.

Mehrabian, Albert. 1998. "Effects of Poll Reports on Voter Preferences." *Journal of Applied Social Psychology* 28 (23): 2119–2130.

Merton, Robert K. 1936. "The Unanticipated Consequences of Purposive Social Action." *American Sociological Review* 1 (6): 894–904.

——. 1938. "Social Structure and Anomie." *American Sociological Review* 3: 672–682. Revised and reprinted in *Social Theory and Social Structure* (New York: Free Press, 1968), 185–214.

——. 1942. "Science and Technology in a Democratic Order." *Journal of Legal and Political Sociology* 1: 15–26. Reprinted as "The Normative Structure of Science" in *The Sociology of Science: Theoretical and Empirical Investiga-*

tions (Chicago: University of Chicago Press, 1973), 267–278.

——. 1948. "The Self-Fulfilling Prophecy." *Antioch Review* (Summer): 193–210. Reprinted in *Social Theory and Social Structure* (New York: Free Press, 1968), 475–490.

——. 1968a. "The Matthew Effect in Science: The Reward and Communication Systems of Science." *Science* 199 (January 5): 55–63.

——. 1968b. "Manifest and Latent Functions." In *Social Theory and Social Structure*, 73–138. New York: Free Press.

——. 1968c. "On Sociological Theories of the Middle Range." In *Social Theory and Social Structure*, 39–72. New York: Free Press.

——. 1973. *The Sociology of Science: Theoretical and Empirical Investigations*, ed. Norman W. Storer. Chicago: University of Chicago Press.

——. 1979. *The Sociology of Science: An Episodic Memoir*. Carbondale, IL: Southern Illinois University Press. Quoted in Robert K. Merton, "Opportunity Structure." In *The Legacy of Anomie Theory*, ed. F. Adler and W.S. Laufer, 2–77. New Brunswick, NJ: Transaction Publishers.

——. 1988. "The Matthew Effect in Science, II: Cumulative Advantage and the Symbolism of Intellectual Property." *Isis* 79: 606–623.

——. 1995a. "Opportunity Structure: The Emergence, Diffusion, and Differentiation of a Sociological Concept, 1930s–1950s." In *The Legacy of Anomie Theory*, ed. Freda Adler and William S. Laufer, 2–78. New Brunswick, NJ: Transaction Publishers.

——. 1995b. "The Thomas Theorem and the Matthew Effect." *Social Forces* 74 (2): 379–422.

——. 1997. "On the Evolving Synthesis of Differential Association and Anomie Theory: A Perspective from the Sociology of Science." *Criminology* 35 (3): 517–525.

——. 1998. "Unanticipated Consequences of Kindred Sociological Ideas: A Personal Gloss." In *Robert K. Merton and Contemporary Sociology,* Carlo Mongardini and Simonetta Tabboni, eds., 295–318. New Brunswick, NJ: Transaction Publishers.

Mills, C. Wright. 1959. *The Sociological Imagination*. London: Oxford University Press.

Moureau, Magdalene. 1987. "Cost and Know-How: The Matthew Effect in Information Retrieval." *Online Review* 11 (6): 355–360.

Murphy, Liam and Thomas Nagel. 2002. *The Myth of Ownership: Taxes and Justice*. New York: Oxford University Press.

Murray, Charles. 2003. *Human Accomplishment*. New York: HarperCollins.

Myrdal, Gunnar. 1939. *Monetary Equilibrium*. London: W. Hodge.

——. 1944. *The American Dilemma*. New York: Harper and Row.

——. 1957. *Rich Lands and Poor*. New York: Harper and Row.

——. 1970. *The Challenge of World Poverty*. New York: Pantheon.

Nasar, Sylvia. 1992. "The 1980s: A Very Good Time for the Very Rich." *New York Times*, March 5, 1Aff.

National Assessment of Educational Progress. 2005. *NAEP 2004 Trends in Academic Progress*. Washington, DC: U.S. Department of Education. Available online at http://nces.ed.gov/nationsreportcard/pdf/main2005/2005463. pdf (accessed July 12, 2008).

National Telecommunications and Information Administration (NTIA). 1999. "Falling Through the Net: Defining the Digital Divide. A Report on the Telecommunications and Information Technology Gap in America. July, 1999." Washington, DC: U.S. Department of Commerce. Available online at http://www.ntia.doc.gov/ntiahome/fttn99/contents.html (accessed August 1, 2008).

Nuttall, Christine. 1996. *Teaching Reading Skills in a Foreign Language*. Oxford: Heinemann.

Oliver, Melvin L. and Thomas M. Shapiro. 1995. *Black Wealth/White Wealth*. New York: Routledge.

——. 2006. *Black Wealth/White Wealth*, 2nd edition. New York: Routledge.

Olson, Alexandra. 2001. "Poverty Summit Has Grim Forecast." *The San Antonio Express-News* (Associated Press), July 14: 23A.

Pager, Devah. 2007. *Marked: Race, Crime and Finding Work in an Age of Mass Incarceration*. Chicago: University of Chicago Press.

Palen, J. John. 2005. *The Urban World*, 7th edition. New York: McGraw-Hill.

Parsons, Talcott. 1951. *The Social System*. Glencoe, IL: Free Press.

Pew Charitable Trusts. 2007. *Pew Internet and American Life Project*. Philadelphia: Pew Charitable Trusts. Available online at http://pewinternet.org/index.asp (accessed August 10, 2008).

Phillips, Kevin. 2002. *Wealth and Democracy*. New York: Broadway Books.

Pickens, T. Boone. 2008. *The First Billion is the Hardest*. New York: Crown.

Piketty, Thomas and Emmanuel Saez. 2003. "Income Inequality in the United States, 1913–1998. *Quarterly Journal of Economics* 118 (February): 1–39.

Postrel, Virginia. 2002. "The Rich Get Richer and the Poor Get Poorer. Right? Let's Take Another Look." *New York Times*, August 15, C2.

Putnam, Robert. 2000. *Bowling Alone: The Collapse and Revival of American Community*. New York: Simon and Schuster.

Rawls, John. 1999. *A Theory of Justice*. Cambridge, MA: Harvard University Press.

Reiman, Jeffrey. 2001. *The Rich Get Richer and the Poor Get Prison*, 6th edition. Boston: Allyn and Bacon. Quoted by permission of the publisher.

Rigney, Daniel. 2001. *The Metaphorical Society*. Lanham, MD: Rowman and Littlefield.

Rosen, Sherwin. 1981. "The Economics of Superstars." *American Economic Review* 71 (5): 845–858.

Rosenthal, Robert and Lenore Jacobson. 1968. *Pygmalion in the Classroom: Teacher Expectation and Pupils' Intellectual Development*. New York: Holt, Rinehart and Winston.

Ross, C.E. and C.L. Wu. 1996. "Education, Age, and the Cumulative Advantage in Health." *Health and Social Behavior* 37 (1): 104–120.

Rossiter, Margaret. 1993. "The—Matthew—Matilda Effect in Science." *Social Studies of Science* 23 (2): 325–341.

——. 1995. *Women Scientists in America*. Baltimore, MD: Johns Hopkins University Press.

Rostow, Walt Whitman. 1960. *The Stages of Economic Growth*. Cambridge: Cambridge University Press.

——. 1980. *Why the Poor Get Richer and the Rich Slow Down*. Austin: University of Texas Press.

Rubin, Zick and Letitia Anne Peplau. 1975. "Who Believes in a Just World?" *Journal of Social Issues* 31 (3): 65–89.

Ryscavage, Paul. 1999. *Income Inequality in America*. Armonk, NY: M.E. Sharpe.

Saez, Emmanuel. 2005. "Top Incomes in the United States and Canada over the Twentieth Century." *Journal of the European Economic Association* 3 (2–3): 402–411.

Sala-i-Martin, Xavier. 2002. "The Disturbing 'Rise' of Global Income Inequality." Working Paper no. 8904. Cambridge, MA: National Bureau of Economic Research. Available online at http://papers.nber.org/papers/W8904 (accessed August 1, 2008).

Salganik, Matthew J., Peter Sheridan Dodds, and Duncan J. Watts. 2006. "Experimental Study of Inequality and Unpredictability in an Artificial Cultural Market." *Science* 10 (February 10): 854–856.

Samuelson, Robert J. 2001. "Indifferent to Inequality? Americans Care Less about the Gap between the Rich and the Poor than about Just Getting Ahead." *Newsweek*, May 7, 45.

———. 2002a. "Trickle-Up Recovery." *Washington Post,* March 6, A19.

———. 2002b. "Debunking the Digital Divide." *Washington Post,* March 20, A33.

Schott, Thomas. 1998. "Ties between Center and Periphery in the Scientific World- System: Accumulation of Rewards, Dominance and Self-Reliance in the Center." *Journal of World-Systems Research* 4 (2): 112–144.

Schumpeter, Joseph. 1942. *Capitalism, Socialism and Democracy.* New York: Harper and Brothers.

Scott, John. 1995. *Sociological Theory: Contemporary Debates.* Brookfield, VT: Edward Elgar.

SEDL (Southwest Educational Development Laboratory). 2001. "Glossary of Reading-Related Terms." Austin, TX: SEDL. Available online at http://www.sedl.org/reading/framework/glossary.html (accessed August 1, 2008).

Selingo, Jeffrey and Jeffrey Brainard. 2006. "Special Report: The Rich-Poor Gap Widens for Colleges and Students." *Chronicle of Higher Education* 52 (April 7): 1ff.

Sen, Amartya. 1997 [1973]. *On Economic Inequality.* New York: Oxford.

Shapiro, Thomas M. 2001. "The Importance of Assets." In *Assets of the Poor,* ed. Thomas M. Shapiro and Edward N. Wolff, 11–33. New York: Russell Sage Foundation.

———. 2004. *The Hidden Cost of Being African American: How Wealth Perpetuates Inequality.* New York: Oxford University Press.

Shaywitz, Bennett A., Theodore R. Holford, John H. Holahan, Jack M. Fletcher, Karla K. Stuebing, David J. Francis, and Sally E. Shaywitz. 1995. "A Matthew Effect for IQ but Not for Reading: Results from a Longitudinal Study." *Reading Research Quarterly* 30 (4): 894–905.

Sherman, Lawrence. 1998. "Policing for Crime Prevention." In *Preventing Crime: What Works, What Doesn't, What's Promising,* Chapter 8. Washington, DC: National Institute for Justice. Available online at http://www.ncjrs.org/works (accessed August 1, 2008).

Shermer, Michael. 2007. *The Mind of the Market.* New York: Henry Holt.

———. 2008. "Why Candidates Really Get Ahead." *Huffington Post,* January 14. Available online at www.huffingtonpost.com/michael-shermer/why-candidates- really-get_b_81392.html (accessed July 4, 2008).

Shipler, David K. 2005. *A Country of Strangers.* New York: Random House.

Simon, Herbert. 1954. "Bandwagon and Underdog Effects and the Possibility of Election Predictions." *Public Opinion Quarterly* 18 (3): 245–253.

Singer, Peter. 1993. *Practical Ethics,* 2nd edition. New York: Cambridge University Press.

———. 2002. *One World: The Ethics of Globalization*. New Haven, CT: Yale University Press.

Skogan, Wesley. 1990. *Disorder and Decline: Crime and the Spiral of Decay in American Neighborhoods*. New York: Free Press.

Sligo, F.X. 1997. "The Matthew Effect in Information Use." *Omega* 25 (3): 301–312.

Sloman, Leon and David W. Dunham. 2004. "The Matthew Effect: Evolutionary Implications." *Evolutionary Psychology*. 2: 92–104.

Smith, Huston. 1991. *The World's Religions*. San Francisco: HarperSanFrancisco.

Smith, R.S. 1999. "Contested Memory: Notes on Robert K. Merton's 'The Thomas Theorem and the Matthew Effect.'" *American Sociologist* 30 (2): 62–77.

Solow, Robert. 1956. "A Contribution to the Theory of Economic Growth." *Quarterly Journal of Economics* 70 (1): 65–94.

Sonnert, Gerhard and Gerald Holton. 1995. *Who Succeeds in Science: The Gender Dimension*. New Brunswick, NJ: Rutgers University Press.

Sowell, Thomas. 2004. *Basic Economics: A Citizen's Guide to the Economy*, expanded and revised edition. New York: Basic Books.

Squires, Gregory, ed. 2004. *Why the Poor Pay More*. Westport, CT: Praeger.

Stanovich, Keith. 1986. "Matthew Effects in Reading: Some Consequences of Individual Differences in the Acquisition of Literacy." *Reading Research Quarterly* 21 (4): 360–407.

———. 1993. "Romance and Reality." *Reading Teacher* 47 (4): 280–291.

Stinchecombe, Arthur. 1968. *Constructing Social Theories*. New York: Harcourt, Brace and World.

Storer, Norman W. 1973. "Prefatory Note." In Robert K. Merton, *The Sociology of Science: Theoretical and Empirical Investigations* (Chicago: University of Chicago Press), 415–418.

Tang, Thomas Li-Ping. 1996. "Pay Differentials as a Function of Rater's Sex, Money Ethic, and Job Incumbent's Sex: A Test of the Matthew Effect." *Journal of Economic Psychology* 17 (1): 127–144.

Thornton, Saranna. 2007. "Annual Report on the Economic Status of the Profession, 2006–7." *Academe* 9 (2): 21–34.

Thurow, Lester. 1980. *The Zero-Sum Society*. New York: Basic.

Toobin, Jeffrey. 2003. "Annals of Law: The Great Election Grab." *New Yorker*, December 8, 63ff.

Trow, Martin. 1984. "The Analysis of Status." In *Perspectives in Higher Education,* ed. Burton C. Clark, 132–164. Berkeley: University of California Press.

Tumin, Melvin. 1953. "Some Principles of Stratification: A Critical Analysis." *American Sociological Review* 18 (4): 387–394.

Turner, Jonathan H. 1984. *Societal Stratification.* New York: Columbia University Press.

United Nations Development Programme. 2002. *Human Development Report.* New York: Oxford University Press.

University of California Atlas of Global Inequality. 2008. "Debate about Income Inequality." Santa Cruz, CA: University of California. Available online at http://ucatlas.ucsc.edu/income/debate.html (accessed August 2, 2008).

Valian, Virginia. 1999. *Why So Slow? The Advancement of Women.* Cambridge, MA: MIT Press.

Veblen, Thorstein. 1915. *Imperial Germany and the Industrial Revolutions.* New York: MacMillan.

Velasco, Andrés. 2002. "The Dustbin of History: Dependency Theory." *Foreign Policy* 133 (November/December): 44–45.

Veugelers, Reinhilde and Katrien Kesteloot. 1996. "Bargained Shares in Joint Ventures among Asymmetric Partners: Is the Matthew Effect Catalyzing?" *Journal of Economics* 64 (1): 23–51.

Walberg, Herbert J. and Shiow-Ling Tsai. 1983. "Matthew Effects in Education." *American Educational Research Journal* 20 (3): 359–373.

Walden, Graham. 1996. *Polling and Survey Research Methods: 1935–1979: An Annotated Bibliography.* Westport, CT: Greenwood Press.

Wallerstein, Immanuel. 1976/1980. *The Modern World System,* 2 vols. New York: Academic.

Wallis, Jim. 2005. *God's Politics.* San Francisco: HarperSanFrancisco.

Watts, Duncan. 2007. "Is Justin Timberlake a Product of Cumulative Advantage?" *New York Times Magazine,* April 15, 22–25.

Weber, Max. 1946 [1922]. "Class, Status and Party." In *From Max Weber,* ed. Hans Gerth and C. Wright Mills, 180–195. Oxford: Oxford University Press.

——. 1958 [1905]. *The Protestant Ethic and the Spirit of Capitalism,* trans. Talcott Parsons. New York: Scribner.

Wiener, Norbert. 1961 [1948]. *Cybernetics,* 2nd edition. Cambridge, MA: MIT Press.

Wilson, William Julius. 1987. *The Truly Disadvantaged*. Chicago: University of Chicago Press.

———. 1996. *When Work Disappears*. New York: Random House.

Wolff, Edward N. 1995/2002. *Top Heavy: The Increasing Inequality of Wealth in America and What Can Be Done About It*. New York: New Press.

Woo, Lillian G., F. William Schweke, and David E. Buchholz. 2004. *Hidden in Plain Sight: A Look at the $335 Billion Federal Asset-Building Budget*. Washington, DC: Corporation for Enterprise Development. Available online at www.cfed.org/publications/Hidden%20in%20Plain%20Sight%20Summary.pdf (accessed August 1, 2008).

World Bank. 2002. *World Development Indicators 2002* (CD-ROM). Washington, DC: World Bank.

Zuckerman, Harriet A. 1965. "Nobel Laureates: Sociological Studies of Scientific Collaboration." Ph.D. dissertation, Department of Sociology, Columbia University.

———. 1968. "Patterns of Name-Ordering among Authors of Papers: A Study of Social Symbolism and its Ambiguity." *American Journal of Sociology* 74 (3): 276–291.

———. 1972. "Interviewing an Ultra-Elite." *Public Opinion Quarterly* 36 (2): 159–175.

———. 1977. *Scientific Elite: Nobel Laureates in the United States*. New York: Free Press.

———. 1987. "Persistence and Change in the Careers of Men and Women Scientists and Engineers." In *Women: Their Underrepresentation and Career Differentials in Science and Engineering*, ed. L.S. Dixon, 123–156. Washington, DC: National Technical Information Services.

———. 1998. "Accumulation of Advantage and Disadvantage: The Theory and Its Intellectual Biography." In *Robert K. Merton and Contemporary Sociology*, ed. C. Mongardini and S. Tabboni, 139–162. New Brunswick, NJ: Transaction.

Zuckerman, Harriet A. and Robert K. Merton. 1972. "Age, Aging, and Age Structure in Science." In *Aging and Society, Vol. 3: A Theory of Age Stratification*, ed. Matilda W. Riley, Marilyn Johnson, and Anne Foner, 292–356. New York: Russell Sage Foundation. Reprinted in Robert K. Merton, *The Sociology of Science: Theoretical and Empirical Investigations* (Chicago: University of Chicago Press, 1973), 497–559.

Zuckerman, Harriet A., Jonathan R. Cole, and John T. Bruer, eds. 1991. *The Outer Circle*. New York: Norton.

INDEX